MORE FROM THE SENSITIVE GOURMET

More
from
the
Sensitive
Gourmet

A WONDERFUL COLLECTION OF
GLUTEN-FREE OR DAIRY-FREE BAKING,
COOKIES AND PUDDINGS

Antoinette
Savill

Thorsons

Thorsons
An Imprint of HarperCollins*Publishers*
77–85 Fulham Palace Road,
Hammersmith, London W6 8JB

The Thorsons website address is:
www.thorsons.com

Published by Thorsons 1999
1 3 5 7 9 10 8 6 4 2

© Antoinette Savill, 1999

Photography by Dave King

Antoinette Savill asserts the moral right to
be identified as the author of this work

A catalogue record for this book
is available from the British Library

ISBN 0 7225 3848 0

Printed and bound in Great Britain by
The Bath Press, Bath

Contents

Acknowledgements

My thanks to Wanda Whiteley for encouraging me to embark on this new collection of healthy recipes specifically for those of us with a sweet tooth! Also to the most important person in my life, Stephen Lawrence who constantly guided, supported and advised me. I couldn't have written and tested all the recipes without the help of Lisa who constantly cleared up after me! Finally, to everyone who has helped me throughout this book.

Foreword

Style and flair in cooking is the secret of a perfect meal. Often the simplest and freshest ingredients make the most effective and delicious food, without any real effort. This is getting far easier as the years go by and more and more wonderful ingredients become readily available.

People are becoming increasingly concerned about what they eat, and so recipes have become more diversified. Those of us who are professional cooks must take the responsibility to adapt and improve our recipes to suit the needs of different generations of people with food intolerances, sometimes using ingredients that are unfamiliar to many, and may even considered by some to be faddish.

After much pressure from the public, the big supermarkets are all selling a greatly increased selection of soya, wheat and gluten-free products to cater for this need.

Thank goodness magazines are now incorporating one or two allergy-free style recipes in some of their issues, and each month the response to these is gradually increasing as people realize that you don't actually have to be ill to benefit from a change in diet. In fact the more varied a diet is, the better it is for you. Different types of flours, sugars and non-dairy liquids are bound to be beneficial in an all-round balanced diet. Too much of anything, however good for you, is not such a healthy thing.

Nobody could predict the leap in food allergies that has unfortunately taken place over the last few years. Instead of being defeated, we should take advantage of this, finding new and exciting ways of eating and enjoying sensitively prepared food with the people we love to be with.

Symbols Used Throughout this Book

The following symbols are very important. They are your guides to what is in each recipe. You can use each recipe with complete confidence knowing that a professional nutritionist has checked each recipe.

 = GLUTEN FREE (Which is wheat free.)

 = WHEAT FREE (Which is not gluten free. However, check the recipe because you may be able to tolerate oats or barley used.)

 = DAIRY FREE (This is lactose free. All non-dairy free recipes use goat or sheep's products, which can be tolerated by most people.)

Any one, or all, of these symbols is printed at the top of each recipe. Please be sure that you are not allergic or intolerant to any other substances in the ingredients.

Introduction

Don't worry if any of the ingredients in the book seem unfamiliar – they are all available at supermarkets, Italian delicatessens or health food shops. If you live some distance from a large town or city and none of these options are available to you then there are marvellous mail order companies around. You will find a helpful list of these on page 136. I have also included my list of ingredients, which might come in useful.

If you are new to this challenging game of food avoidance, the table on page 138 will reassure you. It is an excellent guide, compiled for me by Sir Charles Jessel, Governor of the Institute for Optimum Nutrition, when I started creating recipes to pander to my gastronomic needs.

In my opinion, you only remember the last thing that you ate at any lunch or dinner party. If however, everything is superb then there is even more reason for the pudding to do justice to the rest of the meal. On the other hand, a simple menu with a grand finale of a wickedly luscious pudding will send your guests into a paroxysm of delight and ensure the evening is a success.

All the recipes in this book can be made with dairy and wheat products if you are lucky enough to be restored to perfect health.

A professional nutritionist and home economist has vetted all the recipes for your safety. Different products around the world can vary, so please always read the labels on all of the ingredients. Also, do check the ingredient list before you start shopping and cooking to make sure that you are not intolerant of any of the other items.

The purpose of this cookbook is to allow those with food intolerances to entertain family and friends on all occasions and throughout the various celebrations of the year, giving everyone such delicious food that none will even realize that the ingredients are slightly different. The idea then is to make entertaining, be it a children's tea party or a simple picnic in the garden, a relaxing, fun and sociable few hours for everyone – including the cook!

Sharing food should be a stress-free event, a joy, a healer of the spirit and soul – an all-encompassing pleasure for you and those you enjoy being with.

CHAPTER 1

Breads, Muffins and Scones

To begin with, we should really start with the time when our bodies most need fuel – breakfast! So often neglected, breakfast for many people is little more than a hasty bowl of corn flakes – when remembered at all. My fantastic acupuncturist, Amanda, always tells me that if we had a car there is absolutely no way that we would dream of driving it all day without any oil or petrol. So why do we so often work all morning without giving our minds and bodies precious water and food for energy? Breakfast makes us more alert and much more efficient, so why miss it!

There are some great recipes that can be baked for breakfast, brunch or afternoon tea. In this chapter you will find a tempting choice of breads that should at last make up for the delicious but forbidden ones in the stores. The breads should last up to 3 days if sealed up in airtight containers or bags. I always double up on the loaves that I bake and freeze one of them for the weekdays when I am likely to be constantly battling against time.

Muffins are great breakfast food. They are easy to make and can be kept for a day or two in airtight containers or bags and reheated briefly in a microwave before serving. They also freeze well. Scones and other pancake-type foods are much more temperamental and are better eaten fresh and hot. However, scones can easily be frozen and then reheated briefly in a microwave when you have a craving for one.

Sun-dried Tomato and Coriander Seed Bread

This bread is delicious with soups and starters, and also makes wonderful sandwiches for picnics or your daily lunch box. For a change you can swap the tomatoes to chopped black olives or fried onions. Alternatively, use chopped, stoned (pitted) dates for a sweeter combination.

Makes 2 loaves

455g/1lb/3¼ cups of rye flour

310g/11oz/2¼ cups of The Stamp Collection (WF) flour

1 teaspoon of salt

14g/½oz/1 package of easy-bake (instant) yeast

300ml/10fl oz/1¼ cups of unsweetened apple juice, mixed with the same amount of tepid water

2 tablespoons of black treacle (molasses)

2 tablespoons of finely chopped sun-dried tomatoes

1 tablespoon of coriander seeds

2 greased large non-stick loaf tins, or 2 non-stick trays

Extra flour for kneading dough

Preheat the oven to 200°C/400°F/Gas mark 6

Sift together the flours and the salt in a bowl. Mix in the yeast, then make a well in the dry ingredients and stir in the warm apple juice and water mixture.

Dip a tablespoon into boiling water to heat it and then quickly use the spoon to add the treacle to the warm mixture. Mix until you have a firm dough. Remove the dough from the bowl and knead thoroughly on a lightly floured surface for 8 minutes.

Add the chopped tomatoes and knead the dough for another 2 minutes. Divide the mixture into the 2 non-stick loaf tins, or on to the 2 non-stick trays, cover the dough with clingfilm (plastic wrap) and leave in a warm place until the dough has doubled in size.

Place the dough in the tins on a baking sheet, sprinkle the bread tops with a little water and then gently press in the coriander seeds. Bake in the oven for about 35 minutes.

Allow the loaves to cool slightly, then turn out on to a wire rack to cool completely.

Serve the bread in slices and keep it fresh in sealed polythene bags.

Southern Cornbread

Cornmeal makes glorious golden yellow bread that has a traditional American/Italian flavour seldom used in England. It can be made into savoury bread by changing the pine nuts to onions, herbs, chilli or crispy bacon. The bread is then ideal for soups and salads instead of being a delicious breakfast or tea bread.

Serves 8

70g/2¹/₂oz/¹/₂ cup of rice flour
70g/2¹/₂oz/¹/₂ cup of maize flour
1 tablespoon of (GF) baking powder
140g/5oz/1 cup of quick-cook polenta (maize) or cornmeal
1 teaspoon of salt
340ml/12fl oz/1¹/₂ cups of apple juice
85g/3oz/6 tablespoons of (DF) margarine, melted

2 large free-range eggs, beaten
3 teaspoons of runny honey
200g/7oz/1¹/₄ cups of pine nuts, toasted golden brown under the grill

A greased 23cm/9-inch square, non-stick baking tin or a loaf tin

Preheat the oven to 200°C/400°F/Gas mark 6

Sift together the flours and baking powder in a bowl. Stir in the polenta (maize) and salt and make a well in the centre of the flour.
Beat the apple juice and margarine together in another bowl. Whisk together the eggs and honey in a separate bowl. Add both mixtures to the flour mixture and stir thoroughly. Stir in the pine nuts and tip into the tin.
Bake the cornbread for 30 minutes until well risen and golden brown. Allow the bread to cool, then turn it out on to a wire rack to cool completely.

Walnut Bread

I love sandwiches, but because of my wheat intolerance I can not buy them in the shops, so this is the food I have missed most. It is also the hardest snack to replace for speed and nutrition. Luckily, now I just slice up the loaf and freeze the slices in pairs ready for action!

Serves 8

14g/¹/₂oz/1 package of easy-bake (instant) yeast
1 teaspoon of salt
2 teaspoons of honey
400ml/14fl oz/1³/₄ cups of warm water
2 tablespoons of vegetable oil
500g/17oz/6 cups of porridge oats, processed
   to a fine flour

2 heaped teaspoons of ground cinnamon
A pinch of grated nutmeg
2 tablespoons of chopped walnuts

1 large greased non-stick loaf tin, or non-stick baking
   tray

Preheat the oven to 180°C/350°F/Gas mark 4

Put the yeast, salt and honey in a large bowl. Add the warm water and oil, then mix in the processed oats, cinnamon and nutmeg.
Knead the dough with floured hands on a floured board for 10 minutes. Divide the dough in half and briefly knead in the walnuts. Shape the dough into an oval and place it in the centre of the tray.
Prove the dough in a very warm place for about 30 minutes, allowing it to rise slightly.
Place the dough in either the loaf tin or on the baking tray and bake for 1 hour until the bread is firm.
Cool the bread on a wire rack and when the bread is cold slice and serve.

Double Chocolate Chip Muffins

I have never quite managed to start the day with chocolate, but I have no doubts that to many people it is absolute bliss! However, for pure indulgence, these freshly baked muffins with a large cappuccino are heaven.

Serves 6

140g/5oz/1 cup of rice flour
115g/4oz/³/4 cup of The Stamp Collection (WF) flour
1 heaped tablespoon of (DF) cocoa powder
140g/5oz/³/4 cup of caster (superfine) sugar
1 tablespoon of (GF) baking powder
1 teaspoon of pure Madagascan vanilla extract
2 large free-range egg whites

140ml/5fl oz/²/3 cup of goat's yogurt
90ml/3fl oz/¹/3 cup of (WF) sweetened apple sauce
115g/4oz/²/3 cup of (DF) chocolate chips or chopped dark chocolate

2 × 6 large non-stick muffin trays, lined with paper muffin cases

Preheat the oven to 200°C/400°F/Gas mark 6

In a large bowl, stir together the first six ingredients. Make a well in the centre of the mixture.
In another bowl, beat the egg whites until foamy and then fold in the yogurt and apple sauce. Add this mixture to the dry mixture and stir in the chocolate chips.
Spoon the batter into the tray of muffin cups, filling each one three-quarters full.
Bake the muffins for 20–25 minutes, or until an inserted skewer comes out clean.
Cool them in the tray for about 5–10 minutes before transferring to a wire rack to cool slightly.
Serve the muffins warm.

Date and Walnut Muffins

On our recent trip to America, we stayed in a hotel that had marvellous breakfasts. Baskets of warm and aromatic muffins full of fruit and spices lay waiting for us, how could we resist? We did not and I am still trying to shed the pounds!

Serves 6

115g/4oz/³⁄4 cup of rice flour

115g/4oz/³⁄4 cup of maize flour

2¹⁄2 teaspoons of (GF) baking powder

¹⁄2 fresh nutmeg, finely grated

1 heaped teaspoon of mixed spice (pie spice)

100g/3¹⁄2oz/7 tablespoons of (DF) margarine cut up into pieces

55g/2oz/scant ¹⁄4 cup of caster (superfine) sugar

1 large free-range egg

300ml/10fl oz/1¹⁄4 cups of (DF) natural yogurt or not dairy free sheep or goat's yogurt

60ml/2fl oz/¹⁄4 cup of water

170g/6oz/1 cup of chopped, stoned (pitted) dates

55g/2oz/¹⁄2 cup of walnuts, chopped

Zest of 1 lemon

Demerara sugar for sprinkling

12 paper muffin cases set in a bun/muffin tin for 12

Preheat the oven to 190°C/375°F/Gas mark 5

Sift the flours, baking powder and spices into a mixing bowl. Rub in the margarine with your fingertips until it resembles breadcrumbs, then stir in the sugar.

In another mixing bowl, beat the egg, yogurt and water together. Fold this mixture into the flour mixture using a metal spoon.

Add the chopped dates, walnuts and lemon zest and mix it all together.

Spoon the mixture into the paper cases in the bun tin, sprinkle with demerara sugar and bake for 20 minutes, or until well risen and firm to touch.

Cool the muffins slightly in the paper cases and serve just warm.

Crunchy Nutmeg and Banana Muffins

Mashed banana or grated carrot makes muffins extra moist and if you add (GF) muesli and nuts to the tops then you get a contrasting crunchy bite as well.

Serves 6

240ml/8fl oz/1 cup of sunflower oil

3 large free-range eggs

140g/5oz/^{3}/4 cup of light muscovado sugar

1 large ripe banana, peeled and mashed

140g/5oz/1 cup of grated carrot

1 teaspoon of freshly grated nutmeg

100g/3^1/2oz/^{2}/3 cup of rice flour

100g/3^1/2oz/^{2}/3 cup of maize flour, sifted

2 teaspoons of (GF) baking powder

Demerara sugar for sprinkling

12 paper cases set in a bun/muffin tin for 12

Preheat the oven to 190°C/375°F/Gas mark 5

Beat the oil, eggs, muscovado sugar, mashed banana and grated carrot together and then gently mix in the nutmeg, the flours and the baking powder. Carefully spoon the mixture into paper cases in the bun tin and sprinkle with demerara sugar.

Bake the muffins for 25 minutes, or until they are well risen and cooked through. Leave them to cool slightly in the paper cases and then serve them warm.

Orange and Mincemeat Muffins

This is a great way to use up excess mincemeat left over from the Christmas and New Year festivities.

Serves 6

140g/5oz/1 cup of rice flour

140g/5oz/1 cup of maize flour

2½ teaspoons of (GF) baking powder

2 teaspoons of (GF) bicarbonate of soda (baking soda)

85g/3oz/6 tablespoons of dark muscovado sugar

1 teaspoon of ground cinnamon

A pinch of salt

300ml/10fl oz/1¼ cups of (DF) yogurt or non (DF)

sheep or goat's yogurt

75ml/2½ fl oz/¼ cup of fresh orange juice

Zest of 1 orange

4 tablespoons of sunflower oil

1 large free-range egg

255g/9oz/¾ cup of (GF) luxury mincemeat

12 paper muffin cases to fill a bun/muffin tin for 12

Preheat the oven to 200°C/400°F/Gas mark 6

Sift together the flours, baking powder, bicarbonate of soda (baking soda), sugar, cinnamon and a pinch of salt into a mixing bowl.

In another bowl, mix together the yogurt, orange juice and zest with the oil and egg.

Gently mix the wet ingredients into the dry ingredients using a metal spoon. Add the mincemeat and blend briefly.

Spoon the mixture into the paper cases in the tin and bake for 20 minutes, or until golden and firm.

Leave the muffins to cool in the paper cases and serve them cold.

English Scones

The ultimate treat years ago when I could eat wheat, was to be invited by Rose, who did the PR for the Park Lane hotel, to gossip like mad over a scrumptious afternoon tea in the very grand dining room there. Manners forgotten, every crumb of every scone was scooped up with clotted cream and strawberry jam (jelly) – all in the name of public relations of course!

Serves 6

115g/4oz/³/4 cup of rice flour

115g/4oz/³/4 cup of barley flour

¹/2 teaspoon of salt

1 tablespoon of caster (superfine) sugar

2 teaspoons of (GF) baking powder

55g/2oz/¹/4 cup of (DF) margarine, cut up into pieces

1 large free-range egg, beaten

5 tablespoons of goat's milk

Extra goat's milk to glaze

Preheat the oven to 230°C/450°F/Gas mark 8

Preheat a baking sheet in the oven.

Sift the flours, salt, sugar and baking powder into a large bowl and rub in the margarine until the mixture resembles breadcrumbs.

Make a well in the centre of the dry ingredients and stir in the beaten egg and goat's milk to make a soft dough.

Turn the dough on to a floured surface and knead quickly and lightly to remove any cracks.

Gently flatten the dough with the palm of your hand until it is about 2cm/³/4-inch thick. Using a floured 5cm/2 inch cutter, cut out 5 dough rounds as close to each other as possible. If there are enough trimmings to make another one, then do so.

Carefully place all the rounds on the hot baking sheet and brush them with a little extra milk.

Bake in the centre of the oven for about 8–10 minutes or until they are firm, well risen and golden.

Cool the scones on a wire rack and serve them fresh with lots of jam!

Potato Scones

Years ago, when I cooked in a lodge at Balmoral Castle in Scotland during the fishing season, I was taught to make these griddle scones. I was told firmly never to use old mashed potatoes but to keep it for the salmon fishcakes we would be eating for breakfast every morning!

Serves 4

I large potato or 255g/9oz peeled weight
30g/1oz/2 tablespoons of (DF) margarine
55g/2oz/scant ½ cup of rice flour
½ teaspoon of salt

I teaspoon of (GF) baking powder
Some extra flour for sprinkling
A little oil

Peel the potato, cut it into chunks and cook in boiling water in a saucepan until tender. Drain the potato in a colander until dry, transfer to a bowl and mash with the margarine until light and fluffy. Sift the flour, salt and baking powder into a large bowl and mix in the mashed potato.
Roll the mixture into a ball and turn out on to a lightly floured board. Sprinkle flour on to the rolling pin and the dough and then roll out into a circle, about 5mm/¼-inch thick.
Cut into 8 wedges and prick all over with a fork. Lightly grease a griddle or brush a frying pan with oil and transfer the wedges to it as soon as it is hot.
Cook for 5 minutes on each side, until golden brown and firm.
Cool on a serving plate for 5 minutes before serving with (DF) margarine and a piping hot bowl of soup. For breakfast I suggest serving the potato scones with lashings of (DF) scrambled eggs and crispy bacon or poached eggs and ham.

Welsh Cakes

Now cooked on a griddle, these little Welsh gems would once have been cooked on a bakestone – a hot slab of stone over an open fire. Freshly cooked they need no embellishment, but once they are cold they do need little butter or margarine.

Serves 6

115g/4oz/³/4 cup of rice flour	85g/3oz/6 tablespoons of caster (superfine) sugar
115g/4oz/³/4 cup of millet flour	85g/3oz/¹/2 cup of dried mixed fruit
A pinch of salt	1 free-range egg, beaten
¹/2 teaspoon of mixed spice (pie spice)	1 tablespoon of apple or orange juice
¹/4 teaspoon of mace	Extra caster (superfine) sugar to sprinkle
55g/2oz/¹/4 cup of (DF) margarine	Extra flour for rolling
55g/2oz/¹/4 cup of white fat, cubed	A little oil

Sift the flours, salt and spices into a bowl. Rub in the margarine and white fat until you have a breadcrumb consistency. Stir in the caster sugar and dried mixed fruit, then mix in the egg and juice until you have a light dough.

Using a floured rolling pin, roll the dough out on a floured board until it is about 5mm/¹/4-inch thick, then use a 7.5cm/3 inch pastry cutter to cut out 12 rounds.

Lightly oil a griddle or a frying pan and heat until hot.

Cook the cakes in batches for 4–5 minutes on each side until they are golden brown but still soft in the middle.

Sprinkle with caster (superfine) sugar when they are done and leave to cool slightly on wire racks until ready to eat.

Johnny Cakes and Maple Syrup

This was the height of our American breakfasts on our last visit to see my friends in Greenwich. I have adapted them and when we have time at the weekends, in between wading through piles of newspapers and colour supplements, we devour Johnny cakes with maple syrup and (DF) vanilla ice-cream – a huge sin in the book of calories!

Serves 4 (2 each)

140g/5oz/1 cup of fine (GF) corn meal or fine (GF) polenta (maize)	2 large free-range eggs
100g/3¹/₂oz/²/₃ cup of rice flour	300ml/10fl oz/1¹/₄ cups of goat's milk
4¹/₂ teaspoons of (GF) baking powder	30g/1oz/2 tablespoons of melted (DF) margarine
2 teaspoons of caster (superfine) sugar	Oil for brushing the pan
¹/₂ teaspoon of salt	Maple syrup to serve

Stir together the dry ingredients in a bowl.

Whisk the eggs and goat's milk in a large bowl. Gradually beat in the dry ingredients and, when well combined, stir in the melted margarine.

Heat two oiled griddle or non-stick frying pans and use a tablespoon to drop the batter on to the very hot surface. Make the pancakes about 6cm/2¹/₂ inch in diameter.

Once the base is cooked and golden brown, turn the pancake over and cook the other side until they are cooked through.

Serve the pancakes straight from the griddle on heated plates with lots of maple syrup and your choice of (DF) margarine or butter.

CHAPTER 2

Hot Puddings

The idea of this collection of new recipes is to inspire you to cook and bake again all those tempting treats long avoided on gluten, wheat or dairy-free diets. The heavenly smell of baking wafting through the house is so heart warming and comforting at any time of the year – but especially in the bleak mid-winter.

Every mouthful of sticky chocolate is a seductive pleasure. All part of the rich tapestry of life, which can all too suddenly disappear when, diagnosed with some food based allergy.

Just because certain foods become out of bounds there is no need not to be able to indulge in wonderful puddings. Now you can enjoy the same sort of puddings, just put together differently with alternative ingredients.

I hope this will encourage you to have fun experimenting with lots of ways to make safer, healthier puddings for yourself and your family.

Sweet, hot and pretty has to be the ideal pudding! You can use new contrasting textures and colours to create innovative contemporary puddings to impress your trendy friends. Alternatively, according to your mood, choose the illustrious classic dishes of the past now adapted to the present. Whichever suits your style and palate here is a wide selection for you.

A hot pudding should revive low spirits and warm the body. This is just what is needed to combat the cold months of each year.

Crêpes Suzettes

This year we had the most romantic New Year's Eve in Paris. After a fabulous evening at the ballet, we strolled up the magnificent boulevards, which were full of hooting cars and joyful Parisians, until we reached our favourite restaurant. There, finally at 2am, we had the best crêpes Suzettes in Paris, or maybe that was the effect of the champagne!

Serves 6–8

CRÊPES
55g/2oz/scant ½ cup of rice flour
55g/2oz/scant ½ cup of barley flour
A pinch of salt
3 large free-range eggs
240ml/8fl oz/1 cup of soya milk or (not DF) goat's
   milk mixed with 30g/1oz/2 tablespoons of melted
   (DF) margarine
Sunflower oil for frying

FILLING
115g/4oz/½ cup of (DF) margarine
4 heaped tablespoons of icing (confectioners') sugar
3 tablespoons of strained fresh orange juice
1 tablespoon of grated orange rind
1 tablespoon of Cointreau or orange liqueur
Extra (DF) margarine for frying
Extra caster (superfine) sugar

3 tablespoons of brandy and 3 tablespoons of
   Cointreau or orange liqueur

18cm/7 inch crêpe pan (makes about 12–16 crêpes)
Baking parchment (wax paper)

Make the crêpes first. Sift the flours into a bowl with the salt, make a well in the centre, break the eggs into the well and whisk them until thoroughly mixed.

Add half the milk and melted margarine in a steady stream and whisk, gradually making a smooth paste. Continue whisking as you add the remaining liquid in order to prevent lumps forming. Leave the batter to stand for 30 minutes.

Heat a little of the oil in the frying pan until a drop of the crêpe mixture sizzles and sets quickly. Now ladle a tablespoon of the crêpe mixture into the pan and swirl it around so that the base of the pan is evenly coated. Cook until crispy and golden, then flip over and cook the other side. Continue until you have used up all the batter, layering each crêpe on baking parchment (wax paper) as you go.

Now make the filling by mixing the margarine and icing (confectioners') sugar together in a food processor until pale and light. Add the orange juice and rind with the liqueur and blend just long enough to become smooth.

Spread the filling over each crêpe and fold into a triangle. Heat a little margarine in a large frying pan, add the crêpes and sprinkle with caster (superfine) sugar. Pour over the 3 tablespoons of both the brandy and Grand Marnier and set light to it. Cook until the flames go out and then serve immediately.

MORE FROM THE SENSITIVE GOURMET

Spring Rolls and Passionfruit Sauce

This is such a novel and exotic idea. Fiona, who is also a cook, and I, were perusing the two brand-new food magazines that she had just discovered. We love to discuss recipes and new ideas and eventually I concocted this recipe.

Serves 6 (2 each with a few spare ones)

ROLLS
I heaped teaspoon of ground ginger
340g/12oz/1 ½ cups of drained weight from a can of finely chopped pineapple flesh in natural juices
2 x 50g/2oz packages (GF) rice flour pancakes for spring rolls
Sunflower oil for frying

SAUCE
410g/14oz can of apricot halves in pineapple or natural juices
3 ripe passion fruit, halved with all the seeds scooped out

Fresh basil leaves to decorate, or exotic orchid flowers for special occasions

First, make the sauce by blending half the apricots and half the juice in a blender. You can use the remainder for decorating the serving plates. I slice them and add a little sprig of fresh basil, or an exotic orchid flower.

Mix the passion fruit pulp into the purée and place a spoonful of the passion fruit sauce on each decorated plate.

On another plate, mix the ginger with the chopped pineapple.

Put plenty of oil in a deep saucepan, no less than about 5cm/2 inches deep, so that you can fry the rolls four at a time.

Next, wet two clean tea towels with fresh tap water and wring them out thoroughly. Place individual pancakes flat on one tea towel and cover them with the second towel. After about a minute they will be soft and pliable.

Take a rice pancake and place it on a clean surface. Spoon a line of the pineapple across the paper, about two thirds of the way up it. Pull the top of the pancake over the filling, bring in and tuck in the sides and then roll up as tightly as you can. This will ensure that the filling can not escape and the rolls will not come undone.

Repeat until all the rolls are finished.

Now fry 4 pancakes at a time until they are crispy and golden all over and bobbing on the surface of the oil.

Drain the pancakes with a slotted spoon and let them sit on some kitchen (paper) towels on a plate in a hot oven until they are all ready (be as quick as you can so that they remain crispy).

To ensure maximum crispiness, serve and eat the rolls immediately on the prepared plates.

Rhubarb and Pistachio Crumble

Pistachios are such fun to nibble at when they are fresh in their shells and easy to crack open and pop into one's mouth. A packet of shelled nuts will do perfectly well for this recipe and the pistachios will add a touch of sophistication to the crumble.

Serves 8

600g/1lb 3oz/4¹/₂ cups of fresh trimmed rhubarb, washed and chopped

4 tablespoons of sugar

³/₄ teaspoon of ground cinnamon

2 whole cloves

2 tablespoons of ginger wine or ginger cordial

100g/3¹/₂oz/7 tablespoons of (DF) margarine

85g/3oz/9 tablespoons of rice flour

85g/3oz/1 cup of millet flakes

4 tablespoons of demerara sugar

100g/3¹/₂oz/³/₄ cup of shelled pistachio nuts, roughly chopped

Sugar for sprinkling

Use a large ovenproof pie dish

Preheat the oven to 190°C/375°F/Gas mark 5

Put the rhubarb, sugar, cinnamon, cloves and ginger wine or cordial into a deep pan and cook gently until just soft. Stir occasionally to prevent sticking.

Make the crumble in a bowl by rubbing the margarine into the flour and millet flakes with your fingertips and stirring in the demerara sugar and nuts.

Remove the cloves from the rhubarb and discard.

Spoon the fruit into an ovenproof pie dish, leaving behind the excess juices. Pour the crumble over the fruit and sprinkle the top with the sugar.

Bake for 40 minutes, or until the crumble is crispy and the rhubarb is bubbling up. Serve hot with the Zabaglione recipe on page 29 or some (DF) vanilla ice-cream.

Sun-dried Tomato and Coriander Seed Bread

Crunchy Nutmeg and Banana, and Orange and Mincemeat Muffins

Pineapple Cake

Blackcurrant Rice Surprise

Amaretto Stuffed Peaches

Blinis with Spiced Cherries

Little Toffee Apple Puddings

Strawberry Tarts with Rose Zabaglione

Apricot Soufflé

The professional 'top hat' effect of this soufflé is created by making a circular indentation with a metal spoon in the centre of the soufflé mixture, just before cooking.

Serves 6

SOUFFLÉ

55g/2oz/¼ cup of (DF) margarine

30g/1oz/scant ¼ cup of (GF) cornflour (cornstarch)

3 tablespoons of orange liqueur

310ml/11 fl oz/1⅓ cups of the prepared apricot sauce

4 large free-range egg yolks

Zest of ½ an orange

6 large free-range egg whites

Caster (superfine) sugar and icing (confectioners') sugar for sprinkling

APRICOT SAUCE

255g/9oz/1¼ cups of ready-to-eat dried stoned (pitted) apricots

Sugar to taste

2 tablespoons of orange liqueur

Juice from 1 orange, and zest from ½ of it

Grease a 1½ litre/2 pint/3 US pint soufflé dish with 30g/1oz/2 tablespoons of (DF) margarine and dust with plenty of caster (superfine) sugar.

Preheat the oven to 200°C/400°F/Gas mark 6

First make the sauce. Place the apricots in a saucepan with sugar to taste and add just enough water to cover them. Simmer until soft, then purée in a blender or pass through a sieve until smooth.

Add the orange liqueur, orange zest and the juice. Add as much water as is needed to make the sauce a good pouring consistency. Measure 310ml/11 fl oz/1⅓ cups of the sauce for the soufflé and transfer the rest to a serving jug, cover and keep warm until needed.

Now make the soufflé. Melt the margarine in a large saucepan over medium heat. Stir in the cornflour (cornstarch) until blended and add 3 tablespoons of orange liqueur.

Gradually stir in the measured apricot sauce until the mixture boils. Remove from the heat and beat in the egg yolks and orange zest.

In a large bowl, beat the egg whites until stiff peaks form. Using a metal spoon, fold one tablespoon of the egg whites into the apricot mixture, blending in thoroughly.

Now, quickly and gently, fold in all the remaining egg whites. Fill the prepared soufflé dish with the mixture, make an indentation in the top if you wish, and dust with caster (superfine) sugar. Bake immediately for about 35–45 minutes, or until firm on top and golden brown. Sprinkle with sieved icing (confectioners') sugar and serve immediately with the accompanying sauce.

Rum and Chocolate Bread Pudding

This captures the essence of traditional British food but is transformed into a contemporary dish with the addition of rum and chocolate. Any leftovers can be eaten cold the next day with (DF) vanilla ice-cream.

Serves 6

170g/6oz (about 6 slices) of (GF) white bread,
  (available from health food stores and by mail
  order)
240ml/8fl oz/1 cup of soya cream
100ml/3½fl oz/⅓ cup of soya milk
140g/5oz of (DF) continental dark chocolate
55g/2oz/scant ¼ cup of caster sugar
55g/2oz/¼ cup of (DF) margarine

1 teaspoon of ground cinnamon
5 tablespoons of dark rum
3 large free-range eggs
1 teaspoon of pure Madagascan vanilla extract

Oil a 26cm/10½ inch x 19cm/7½ inch x 5cm/2 inch
  ovenproof dish

Preheat the oven to 180°C/350°F/Gas mark 4

Remove the crusts from the bread and cut the bread squares into triangles. Put the soya cream and milk, chocolate, sugar, margarine and cinnamon into a bowl. Place the bowl over a pan of simmering water until the sugar has dissolved and the mixture melted. Stir in the rum.
In a separate bowl, whisk the eggs and pour them into the chocolate mixture. Add the vanilla and whisk the eggs again.
Spoon one third of the mixture into the dish and arrange the bread triangles over it, overlapping and pointed side up. Pour in the remainder of the chocolate mixture and, using a wooden spoon, gently press down the bread to ensure that all the bread is submerged.
Leave to stand for 2 hours and then transfer it to the refrigerator for 4 hours. Keep the bowl covered with clingfilm (plastic wrap).
Pour some water into a shallow baking tin and stand the bread and butter pudding dish in it. Bake for 40–45 minutes until puffed up in the centre.
Allow to stand for 10 minutes before eating.

Pear and Blackberry Eve's Pudding

I am so glad that blackberries are being cultivated for supermarkets now, as they are fiendishly difficult to pick amidst all the prickly brambles that grow in the ditches and along windy country lanes. Alas, they are usually covered in exhaust fumes as well!

Serves 8

2 x 425g/15oz cans of pears in natural juice
340g/12oz/2½ cups of fresh or frozen blackberries
½ teaspoon of mixed spice (pie spice)
140g/5oz/½ cup plus 2 tablespoons of (DF) margarine
140g/5oz/¾ cup of light brown sugar
70g/2½oz/½ cup of barley flour

70g/2½oz/½ cup of rice flour
55g/2oz/⅔ cup of ground almonds
2 large free-range eggs, beaten
2 tablespoons of the drained pear juice
2 teaspoons of (GF) baking powder
2 tablespoons of pine nuts

Preheat the oven to 190°C/375°F/Gas mark 5

Drain the pears, reserving two tablespoons of the juice for the pudding. Slice the pears and arrange them in a large ovenproof baking dish. Cover with the blackberries and sprinkle with the mixed spice (pie spice).

In a food processor, beat the margarine with the brown sugar until light and fluffy. Add the flours and ground almonds and briefly combine. Mix the eggs and pear juice together in a small bowl and then blend them briefly into the flour mixture. Finally, fold in the baking powder and gently spread the mixture over the fruit.

Sprinkle the pudding with the pine nuts and bake in the oven for about 40–50 minutes, or until the sponge is browned and just firm to touch.

Serve the pudding hot with (DF) ice-cream or the Zabaglione recipe on page 29.

Greengage and Almond Tart

This sweet, golden green fruit fuses all the late summer flavours together. Ambrosial when ripe, and a much neglected rival to the plum, they are worthy of the highest esteem from the severest critic.

Serves 10

PASTRY
115g/4oz/½ cup of (DF) margarine
55g/2oz/¼ cup of caster (superfine) sugar
1 large free-range egg, beaten
70g/2½oz/½ cup of rice flour
70g/2½oz/½ cup of maize flour
½ teaspoon of ground cinnamon
½ teaspoon of ground allspice
A pinch of salt
1 heaped tablespoon of millet flakes

ALMOND CREAM
85g/3oz/6 tablespoons of (DF) margarine
85g/3oz/6 tablespoons of caster (superfine) sugar

2 large free-range eggs
1 tablespoon of dark rum
85g/3oz/1 cup of ground almonds
20g/¾oz/2 generous tablespoons of rice flour

FRUIT FILLING
680g/1½lb of fresh and very ripe greengages, stalks
    removed
4 tablespoons of apricot jam (jelly) warmed in a pan
    with 1 tablespoon of dark rum

Grease and flour a 32cm/12½ inch loose-bottomed,
    fluted, tart tin

Preheat the oven to 200°C/400°F/Gas mark 6

First make the pastry. Beat the margarine and the sugar together in a food processor and add enough egg to make a wet paste. Sift the flours, spices and salt into the dough, add the millet flakes and process briefly in order to blend together. When the dough comes together into a ball, wrap it in clingfilm (plastic wrap) and chill for 30 minutes in the deep freeze.
Roll out the pastry on a floured board and carefully line the tin with it. You may have to push the pastry into shape with floured fingers. Trim the edges with a knife and discard the remnants.
Now make the cream. Beat the margarine and sugar until pale and fluffy, then mix in the eggs and rum. Fold in the almonds, sieve in the flour and mix gently. Cover the base of the tart with the mixture.
Halve the greengages, remove the stones and arrange the fruit close together all over the almond cream.
Bake the tart for 45 minutes, or until the fruit is puffy and golden. The fruit should be just soft but not bursting.
Remove the tart from the oven and leave it in the tin to cool.

Quickly dissolve the jam and rum together in a small bowl in the microwave and then spread it all over the fruit tart.

Leave the tart to cool before removing it from the tin onto a plate. Serve the tart just warm. You can reheat the tart if you are making it in advance, but it should be served fresh and warm.

Pineapple Cake

Thai food has brought lemon grass to our attention and now we can not get enough of it. Use canned pineapple if you are short of time, but make sure it is in natural fruit juices, otherwise the pudding becomes too sweet and bland. If you prefer a richer taste use dark rum in place of the white.

Serves 8

CAKE	SYRUP AND DECORATION
170g/6oz/¾ cup of (DF) margarine, plus extra for greasing	2 sticks of fresh lemon grass, trimmed of tough outer layer and ends
170g/6oz/¾ cup of caster (superfine) sugar	30g/1oz/2 tablespoons of granulated sugar
Finely grated rind of 1 lemon	Juice of 1 lemon
3 large free-range eggs, separated	3 tablespoons of white rum
85g/3oz/9 tablespoons of rice flour	1 large ripe pineapple, peeled and trimmed, cut into quarters, cored and chopped into slices
75ml/2½floz/¼ cup total combined mixture of the above lemon, juiced and some white rum	Sunflower oil for frying the pineapple
85g/3oz/1 cup of ground almonds	
1 teaspoon of (GF) baking powder	Grease a 22cm/8¾ inch non-stick ring mould cake tin

Preheat the oven to 170°C/325°F/Gas mark 3

Beat the margarine and caster sugar in a food processor until pale and fluffy. Add the finely grated lemon rind to the mixture. Gradually beat in the egg yolks, followed by 2 tablespoons of the flour and the lemon juice and rum mixture. Transfer the mixture to a large bowl and lightly fold in half of the almonds and half the remaining flour.

Now fold in the remaining almonds, the last of the flour and the baking powder. Whisk the egg whites in another bowl until they form firm peaks. Quickly fold the egg whites into the prepared mixture.

Spoon the mixture into the tin and bake in the oven for about 50 minutes, or until an inserted skewer comes out clean.

Allow the cake to cool slightly, then turn it out on to a wire rack to cool completely.

While the cake is baking, slice the lemon grass very finely and place in a pan with the 30g/1oz/2 tablespoons of sugar and 200ml/7fl oz/¾ cup of water. Simmer for 10 minutes over low heat to infuse.

Increase the heat to high, bring the syrup to the boil for 2 or 3 minutes and then add the lemon juice and the rum. Strain the syrup and discard the lemongrass.

Place the cake on to a large serving dish, prick small holes all over the cake and pour the syrup all over the cake.

Just before serving, fry the pineapple slices in the sunflower oil. (If you use a chargrill pan the slices will have trendy grill marks on them). They should be just softened with a few char marks.
Pile the hot pineapple into the central hole of the cake and serve immediately.

Maple and Pumpkin Pie

A perfect pudding to serve on Guy Fawkes night or Hallowe'en. You can make it the day before and heat it up. Serve with (DF) vanilla ice-cream and all the children will be happy too.

Serves 8–12

PASTRY

1 heaped tablespoon of icing (confectioners') sugar

A pinch of salt

70g/2½oz/½ cup of rice flour

70g/2½oz/½ cup of millet flour

70g/2½oz/½ cup of maize flour

140g/5oz/⅔ cup of (DF) margarine, cut into small pieces

1 large free-range egg, beaten

FILLING

200ml/7fl oz/¾ cup of apple juice

1 tablespoon of (GF) cornflour (cornstarch)

425g/15oz/scant 2 cups canned pumpkin

2 large free-range eggs

4 tablespoons of maple syrup

1½ teaspoons of mixed spice (pie spice)

1½ teaspoons of ground cinnamon

A little extra caster (superfine) sugar to sprinkle over the pie

Grease a non-stick, loose-bottomed 23cm/9 inch pie or flan tin

Preheat the oven to 200°C/400°F/Gas mark 6

Mixing the first 5 pastry ingredients in a food processor, add the margarine and blend briefly, before adding the egg to bind it all together.

Roll out the pastry and line the prepared tin. Trim off the excess pastry and keep for decorations.

Mix the apple juice and the cornflour (cornstarch) together in a small bowl. Put the pumpkin into a large bowl and stir in the apple juice mixture, followed by the eggs, maple syrup and spices.

Spoon the mixture into the pastry case and level it off.

Roll out the remaining pastry, cut out pretty little decorations from it and arrange over the filling.

Sprinkle the pastry on top of the pie with a little extra caster (superfine) sugar and bake the pie for about 35 minutes until the filling is firm and set and the pastry is golden brown.

Serve the pie warm.

Blueberry Sponge Pudding with Zabaglione

Steamed sponge puddings have been back in vogue for a few years now. This very traditional English family pudding is economical and easy to make – perfect for the harassed parent battling his or her way through the preparations for Sunday lunch. Here the pudding is served with Zabaglione, but for an even simpler accompaniment try golden syrup (corn syrup).

Serves 8

4 heaped tablespoons of blueberry jam (jelly)

255g/9oz/1¾ cups of fresh blueberries, washed and dried

100g/3½oz/7 tablespoons of (DF) margarine

100g/3½oz/7 tablespoons of caster (superfine) sugar

2 large free-range eggs, beaten

1 teaspoon of pure Madagascan vanilla extract

100g/3½oz/⅔ cup of rice flour

100g/3½oz/⅔ cup of maize flour

2 teaspoons of (GF) baking powder

Apple juice to mix

Greased non-stick paper (wax paper) and some string

Grease a 900ml/1½ pints/3¾ cups pudding basin with (DF) margarine and (GF) flour.

ZABAGLIONE

4 large free-range egg yolks

70g/2½oz/⅓ cup of caster (superfine) sugar

100ml/3½fl oz/⅓ cup of Marsala

First make the pudding. Half fill a large saucepan with water and put it on to boil.

Spoon half the jam (jelly) into the bottom of the prepared pudding basin, cover with half of the blueberries and then spoon on the remaining jam (jelly).

Cream together the margarine and sugar in a food processor for 1 minute. Add the eggs and vanilla and process briefly. Briefly blend in the flours and baking powder. Add the apple juice to soften it to a dropping consistency and fold in the remaining blueberries.

Scrape the mixture immediately into the pudding basin. Cover with greased baking parchment (wax paper), making a central pleat in the paper to allow the pudding to expand.

Secure the paper by tying string firmly around the rim of the bowl, making a little handle so you can lift the pudding out of the water more easily.

Steam, with the saucepan tightly covered, for 1½ hours (topping up the water level when necessary). Carefully lift the pudding our of the saucepan and leave it to settle whilst you make the Zabaglione.

Fill another saucepan one third of the way up with water and bring it to the boil. Put the egg yolks and sugar into a large heatproof bowl and beat together with an electric whisk. Now add the

Marsala. Put the bowl over the saucepan of simmering water and whisk on high speed until very thick. Serve immediately.

Turn the blueberry pudding out on to a large serving plate and serve immediately with the warm sauce.

Blackcurrant Rice Surprise

Nursery puddings, although we hate to admit it, are so very reassuring! Now that trendy restaurants are serving old-fashioned puddings once again, we can all enjoy them.

Serves 6

30g/1oz/2 tablespoons of (DF) margarine
300ml/10fl oz/1 1/4 cups of coconut milk
300ml/10fl oz/1 1/4 cups of soya milk
300ml/10fl oz/1 1/4 cups of water
100g/3 1/2oz/1/2 cup of pudding rice
30g/1oz/2 tablespoons of caster (superfine) sugar

255g/9oz/1 3/4 cups of fresh or frozen trimmed blackcurrants
3 tablespoons of caster (superfine) sugar
3 large free-range eggs, separated
1 teaspoon of pure Madagascan vanilla extract
100g/3 1/2oz/1/2 cup of caster (superfine) sugar

Preheat the oven to 180°C/350°F/Gas mark 4

Melt the margarine with the coconut milk and soya milk in a non-stick saucepan over low heat. Add the water, rice and 30g/1oz/2 tablespoons of caster (superfine) sugar, and increase the heat to medium. Bring the pan of rice to the boil, stirring occasionally, and continue to simmer over lower heat for about 45 minutes until just soft, thick and creamy.
Meanwhile, mix the fruit and 3 tablespoons of sugar together.
Once the rice is done, remove from the heat and stir in the egg yolks and vanilla. Spoon the rice into a deep-sided, ovenproof dish big enough for six servings and level it off. Spoon all the sweetened blackcurrants over the rice.
Make the meringue topping by whisking the egg whites in a large bowl until stiff and then folding in the 100g/31/2oz/1/2 cup of caster (superfine) sugar. Spread gently over the blackcurrants and bake for about 30 minutes, or until well browned.
Serve the pudding either hot or warm.

Nectarine and Apricot Clafoutis

You can vary the fruit in this recipe throughout the year, using fresh or canned and drained, apricots, cherries, blackberries or prunes. Serve warm rather than hot.

Serves 8

3 ripe nectarines, peeled, stoned (pitted) and cut
   into sixths
Juice of ½ a lemon
Icing (confectioners') sugar to dust

BATTER
20g/³/₄oz/3 tablespoons of rice flour
A pinch of salt
115g/4oz/½ cup plus 1 tablespoon of caster

(superfine) sugar
60ml/2fl oz/¼ cup of Amaretto liqueur
Grated rind of 1 lemon
4 large free-range eggs
240ml/8fl oz/1 cup of soya cream

Plenty of (DF) margarine and rice flour for greasing
   and dusting a deep ovenproof china dish about
   28cm/11 inch × 20cm/8 inch

Preheat the oven to 190°C/375°F/Gas mark 5

Put the nectarines and the lemon juice in a bowl together. Make the batter by blending the flour, salt, sugar, liqueur and lemon rind together in a bowl. Gradually incorporate the eggs, followed by the cream.
Shake the excess flour off the prepared dish and arrange the nectarines over the base of the dish.
Mix the remaining lemon juice into the batter and then pour it over the fruit.
Bake in the oven for 40 minutes, or until firm and golden.
Dust the Clafoutis with icing (confectioners') sugar to serve.

Apple and Cranberry Streusel Pudding

The combinations of fruits used in restaurants can be illuminating but also sometimes a little too precious! This is a traditional and festive mixture of fruits, perfect for our bleak mid-winter. Use ripe pears instead of the apples for a change.

Serves 6

140g/5oz/²/₃ cup of (DF) margarine
140g/5oz/³/₄ cup of caster (superfine) sugar
2 large free-range eggs, beaten
Finely grated zest and juice of 1 lemon
70g/2¹/₂oz/¹/₂ cup of barley flour
55g/2oz/scant ¹/₂ cup of oat flour (finely process flaked oats if necessary)
2 teaspoons of (GF) baking powder
45g/1¹/₂oz/¹/₂ cup of ground almonds

TOPPING

3 large dessert apples, peeled, quartered, cored and sliced
255g/9oz/2¹/₄ cups of fresh or frozen cranberries
115g/4oz/¹/₂ cup of soft brown sugar
70g/2¹/₂oz/¹/₂ cup of oat flour
55g/2oz/²/₃ cup of ground almonds
55g/2oz/¹/₄ cup of sunflower margarine
Finely grated zest of 1 lemon
1 heaped teaspoon of ground cinnamon
¹/₂ teaspoon of grated nutmeg
¹/₂ teaspoon of ground cardamom

Grease a 23cm/9 inch loose-bottomed cake tin with some extra margarine

Preheat the oven to 190°C/375°F/Gas mark 5

Cream the margarine and sugar in a food processor and gradually beat in the eggs. Transfer to a bowl, mix in the lemon zest and fold in the flours and baking powder. Gently stir in the ground almonds and lemon juice and then spread the mixture lightly over the bottom of the cake tin. To make the topping, toss the apples and cranberries with 70g/2¹/₂oz/5 tablespoons of the soft brown sugar in a bowl. Spread the fruit over the cake base. Put the remaining soft brown sugar, flour and ground almonds into a bowl and rub in the margarine. Mix in the lemon zest and spices, and spread the mixture over the fruit.
Bake for about 1¹/₂ hours, or until the apples are soft and the streusel browned and crunchy.

Amaretto Stuffed Peaches

Amaretto always brings a smile to my face, as it conjures up memories of sitting on the balcony of our hotel on the Amalfi Coast gazing at the glittering sea and moonlight, sipping a chilled glass of this almond nectar.

Serves 6

6 ripe peaches

Juice of ½ large lemon mixed with treble its quantity of cold water

Juice of 1 large orange and double its quantity of cold water

3 tablespoons of Cointreau mixed with 6 tablespoons of boiling water

55g/2oz/¾ cup of 100% rye breadcrumbs

100g/3½oz of (WF) ratafias (dessert macaroons)

3 tablespoons of Amaretto di Saronno liqueur

Plenty of caster (superfine) sugar

Preheat the oven to 190°C/375°F/Gas mark 5

Wipe the peaches, cut them in half and remove their stones.

Pour the lemon and water mixture and the orange and water mixture into a large ovenproof dish. Neatly arrange the peaches (with the cavities facing up) in the dish and pour over the Cointreau and water mixture, ensuring some of it settles in the peach cavities.

Put the breadcrumbs, ratafias and Amaretto liqueur into a food processor and blend briefly until it forms a wet crumbly mixture.

Spoon the mixture loosely into the peach cavities.

Sprinkle the peaches with plenty of caster (superfine) sugar and bake for 45 minutes, or until the peaches are just soft but still holding their shape.

Serve the peaches warm on their own or with your choice of (DF) ice-cream or the Zabaglione recipe on page 29.

Chocolate Pecan Pie

Pecan pie is always a success whenever it is served, so imagine the impact of a gooey chocolate one! Serve with (DF) vanilla ice-cream for a perfect contrast.

Serves 8

PASTRY

155g/5½oz/1 cup plus 2 tablespoons of rice flour

30g/1oz/2 tablespoons of caster (superfine) sugar

55g/2oz/⅔ cup of ground almonds

85g/3oz/6 tablespoons of (DF) margarine, cut into pieces

1 large free-range egg

2 teaspoons of lemon juice

FILLING

55g/2oz/¼ cup of (DF) margarine

3 tablespoons of (GF& DF) cocoa powder

300ml/10fl oz/1¼ cups of golden syrup (corn syrup)

3 large free-range eggs

85g/3oz/6 tablespoons of soft dark brown sugar

2 tablespoons of rum

170g/6oz/1½ cups of shelled pecan nuts

Grease and line with baking parchment (wax paper) a non-stick, loose-bottomed, 24cm/9½ inch flan tin.

Preheat the oven to 180°C/375°F/Gas mark 4

Place the first four pastry ingredients into a food processor and mix briefly until it resembles crumbs. Add the egg and lemon juice and process for a second or two only. Bring the mixture together using a spatula, wrap the pastry in clingfilm (plastic wrap) and chill for 2 hours.

Roll out the pastry on a floured board and then line the prepared tin with it. Prick all over the pastry base with a fork.

Make the filling by gently melting the margarine in a saucepan and stirring in the cocoa and golden syrup (corn syrup).

Beat the eggs with the brown sugar and rum in another bowl. Stir this into the syrup mixture and add the nuts.

Pour the mixture into the pie shell and bake for 40 minutes, or until the filling is just set and the pastry is golden.

Serve warm with (DF) ice-cream.

Chocolate Topsy Turvy Pudding

This wonderful concoction is a scientific mystery, the chocolate sauce on top of the cake magically sinks down and appears as a sauce at the bottom of the cake. My God-children love it!

Serves 6

100g/3¹/₂oz/²/₃ cup of rice flour

1 heaped teaspoon of (GF) baking powder

5 tablespoons of (DF) cocoa powder

A pinch of salt

55g/2oz/¹/₂ cup of chopped walnuts

115g/4oz/¹/₂ cup of (DF) margarine

115g/4oz/¹/₂ cup plus 1 tablespoon of caster (superfine) sugar

2 large free-range eggs

1 teaspoon of Madagascan vanilla extract

115g/4oz/¹/₂ cup plus 1 tablespoon of soft brown sugar

4 tablespoons of rum

240ml/8fl oz/1 cup of boiling water

Grease a 1¹/₂ litre/2 pint/3 US pint soufflé dish with extra (DF) margarine and dust with a little caster (superfine) sugar.

Preheat the oven to 190°C/375°F/Gas mark 5

Sift the flour, baking powder, 1 tablespoon of the cocoa powder and the salt into a bowl, then fold in the walnuts.

In another large bowl, beat the margarine and sugar until pale and light, add the eggs and vanilla and then briefly mix in the sifted dry ingredients.

Spoon the mixture into the prepared soufflé dish and level off.

Mix the brown sugar with the remaining cocoa and the rum, and dissolve them with the boiling water.

Pour the sauce over the cake and then bake for 30–35 minutes, or until the sponge is just firm and the sauce has sunk to the bottom.

Serve warm on its own or with (DF) vanilla ice-cream.

Plum Tatin

Luckily, this recipe exploits the virtues of unripe plums. As supermarkets seldom seem to sell fruit that is ripe enough, it is the perfect solution.

Serves 6

PASTRY
100g/3¹/₂oz/²/₃ cup of rice flour
70g/2¹/₂oz/¹/₂ cup of maize flour
55g/2oz/¹/₃cup of ground rice
140g/5oz/²/₃ cup (DF) margarine
55g/2oz/¹/₄ cup of caster (superfine) sugar
1 free-range egg, beaten

TOPPING
130g/4¹/₂oz/ ¹/₂ cup plus 1 tablespoon of (DF) margarine
130g/4¹/₂oz/generous ¹/₂ cup of caster (superfine) sugar mixed with 1 tablespoon of ground cinnamon
1kg/2lb 2oz of Victoria plums, wiped clean

Tart Tatin mould or a 25cm/10 inch non-stick, round baking tin

Preheat the oven to 200°C/400°F/Gas mark 6

First make the pastry. Sift the flours and the ground rice together into a large bowl and rub in the margarine until the mixture resembles fine breadcrumbs. Stir in the sugar, add the egg and mix until you have a binding dough. Wrap in clingfilm (plastic wrap) and chill until needed.
Melt the margarine for the topping in a large frying pan with the sugar and cinnamon. Halve the plums and remove the stones. Place the plums in the frying pan and increase the heat to high. Cook the plums until the margarine and sugar starts to caramelize. Quickly remove the pan from the heat and transfer the fruit and juices to the tatin dish.
Roll out the pastry on a floured surface into a thick circle large enough to fit over the plums. Lay the pastry over the fruit and press down slightly.
Bake in the oven for 25–30 minutes, or until the pastry is golden and the fruit cooked and bubbling.
Serve warm with (DF) vanilla ice-cream.

Blinis with Spiced Cherries

You can play around with blinis, using them with other ingredients at other meals throughout the year. They are ideal for brunch parties, served with smoked salmon and goat's cheese. In summer, serve them with raspberries and (DF) vanilla ice-cream.

Serves 6 (2 each)

SPICED CHERRIES

30g/1oz/2 tablespoons (DF) margarine

2 x 850g/1lb 14oz cans of pitted black cherries or a jar of cherries in liqueur if you are in a real hurry!

1 teaspoon of ground cinnamon

30g/1oz/2 tablespoons of caster (superfine) sugar or to taste

Juice and zest of 1 orange

2 tablespoons of Kirsch liqueur

BLINIS

55g/2oz/generous ½ cup of buckwheat flour

55g/2oz/½ cup of rice flour

1 teaspoon of (GF) baking powder

1 teaspoon of olive oil

30ml/1fl oz/2 tablespoons of sunflower oil

2 medium free-range eggs, beaten

140ml/5fl oz/⅔ cup of water

A drop of extra oil for frying

(DF) vanilla ice-cream or alternatively crème fraiche, which is not dairy-free

---

Melt the margarine in a frying pan, add the cherries, cinnamon, sugar, orange juice and zest, and cook for a couple of minutes over medium heat. Add the Kirsch and simmer for about 5 minutes. Keep warm whilst you make the blinis.

Sift the flours with the baking powder into a bowl, make a well in the centre and pour in the oils and eggs. Stir with a balloon whisk and gradually incorporate the water.

Leave the batter to stand at room temperature for 15 minutes.

Heat a large, non-stick frying pan with a drop of extra oil until very hot. Pour a spoonful of the blini mixture into the pan and repeat until you have 4 blinis, each about 6.5cm/2½ inch in diameter.

Cook the blinis until they are firm on the underside and bubbling on the upper side, then turn them over and cook the other side.

Keep the blinis warm until they are all ready.

Serve two of them, overlapping, on each warm plate with a pool of warm spiced cherries beside them and a scoop of (DF) vanilla ice-cream on the edge of the pancakes.

Festive Apple and Mincemeat Meringue

This is an excellent alternative to slaving over heaps of mince pies at Christmas and avoids the hassle of making lots of pastry.

Serves 8

1kg/2.2lb of large cooking apples, washed and dried
1 heaped teaspoon of ground cinnamon
Grated zest of 1 lemon
55g/2oz/4 tablespoons of dark brown sugar
2 tablespoons of Calvados or brandy
825g/1lb 13oz/2½ cups of deluxe (GF& DF) vegetarian mincemeat

4 large free-range egg whites
A pinch of salt
200g/7oz/1 cup of caster (superfine) sugar
55g/2oz/⅔ cup of ground almonds
55g/2oz/⅔ cup of flaked almonds
Ground cinnamon and icing (confectioners') sugar sifted together to dust

Preheat the oven to 150°C/300°F/Gas mark 2

Peel and core the apples, chop up into little cubes and place in a saucepan with the cinnamon, lemon zest, brown sugar and Calvados. Cook for 5 minutes over medium heat, stirring frequently so that the apples do not stick to the pan.

Transfer the mixture to a deep ovenproof dish and level off the top. Spread the mincemeat evenly over the apples.

In a large bowl, whisk the egg whites and salt at high speed until stiff peaks form. Reduce the speed to low and whisk in the 200g/7oz/1 cup of sugar. When the meringue is firm and glossy, gently fold in the ground almonds. Pile the meringue over the mincemeat.

Sprinkle with the flaked almonds and bake for 30–40 minutes until golden and crisp.

Serve dusted with cinnamon and icing (confectioners') sugar.

Christmas Pudding

This pudding was included in my first Sensitive Gourmet book, but it can be made up to one week in advance, which is so useful during the chaotic run-up to Christmas day, that I felt I had to include it again.

Makes 1 very large, or 2 medium puddings

70g/2¹/₂oz/¹/₃ cup of glacé cherries, chopped
170g/6oz/1 cup of candied peel, chopped
340g/12oz/2¹/₂ cups of raisins
170g/6oz/1¹/₄ cups of sultanas (golden raisins)
170g/6oz/1¹/₄ cups of currants
70g/2¹/₂oz/¹/₂ cup of blanched almonds, chopped
255g/9oz/2 cups of 100% (GF) corn breadcrumbs or (WF) Rye breadcrumbs
255g/9oz/2 cups of (GF) shredded vegetarian suet
2 heaped teaspoons of ground cinnamon
2 heaped teaspoons ground mixed spice (pie spice)
¹/₂ of a nutmeg, grated

¹/₂ teaspoon of ground cloves
1 teaspoon of allspice
6 large free-range eggs
Grated rind and juice of 1 orange
Grated rind of ¹/₂ a lemon
140ml/5fl oz/²/₃ cup of Armagnac or brandy
3 tablespoons of rum
Sunflower oil for greasing

Generously oil a 2 litre/3¹/₄ pint/2 quarts pudding basin, or 2 × 1 litre/1³/₄ pint/1 quart basins

Put the dried fruit, almonds, breadcrumbs, suet and spices into a large bowl and mix together. Whisk the eggs until fluffy and thickened, then stir into the dry ingredients. Blend in the grated orange and its juice, the grated lemon and spirits. The mixture should just drop off the spoon. Put the mixture into the pudding basin(s) and smooth over the top. Cover the basin with a layer of oiled foil, double folded in the centre, and secure with string.

Stand the basin on an inverted saucer or a piece of foil folded 4 times, in a very large saucepan. Fill three quarters of the way up with water, cover with a lid or foil and steam for 6¹/₂ hours for a large pudding or 4¹/₂ hours for a smaller one. Top up with boiling water whenever necessary.

When cooked, lift the basin out of the pan and allow to cool. Store in a cool dark place.

To reheat, replace the old foil with new foil and steam for 1¹/₂–2 hours before serving. Serve with Zabaglione recipe on page 29, or Ginger Custard recipe on page 41.

Mince Pies and Ginger Custard

Commercial mincemeat is often too sweet and has a less distinctive texture than home-made. This version is fresh and fruity and can be made anytime from a couple of months before Christmas, to the day before. It's another recipe that was in my first book, but I felt was good enough to repeat.

Makes 48 pies

 or

PASTRY

310g/11oz/scant 2¼ cups of (GF) maize flour or
    millet flour

310g/11oz/scant 2¼ cups of rice flour

310g/11oz/scant 2¼ cups of finely processed (WF)
    oats, or (GF) maize or millet flour (use the opposite
    of the first ingredient choice)

480g/17oz/2¼ cups of (DF) margarine

½ teaspoon of salt

2 large free-range eggs, beaten

Some water to bind the dough

FINISHING TOUCHES

Caster (superfine) sugar and ground cinnamon for
    dusting

Icing (confectioners') sugar

MINCEMEAT

1.5kg/3.3lb/4½ cups of commercial vegetarian
    (GF/DF) mincemeat

or

170g/6oz/1¼ cups of currants

170g/6oz/1¼ cups of raisins, chopped finely

170g/6oz/1¼ cups of sultanas (golden raisins),
    chopped finely

115g/4oz/⅔ cup of prunes, chopped finely

170g/6oz/1 cup of dried apples, chopped finely

115g/4oz/⅔ cup of glacé cherries, chopped finely

115g/4oz/⅔ cup of candied peel, chopped finely

250g/8½oz/2 cups of (GF) vegetarian suet

300g/10½oz/1½ cups of light brown muscovado
    sugar

1 teaspoon of ground cloves

2 teaspoons of mixed spice (pie spice)

Grated rind and juice of 2 lemons

240ml/8fl oz/1 cup of Grand Marnier

Grated rind of 1 orange

1 ripe pear, peeled, cored and chopped

115g/4oz/⅔ cup of fresh cranberries, chopped

GINGER CUSTARD

For 6–8 people (double the quantities for 12–16
    people)

6 large free-range egg yolks

100g/3½oz/½ cup of caster (superfine) sugar

1 tablespoon of (GF) cornflour (cornstarch)

3 tablespoons of stem ginger syrup

570ml/20fl oz/2½ cups of unsweetened soya milk

3 tablespoons of Stones' ginger wine, or rum

Preheat the oven to 180°C/350°F/Gas mark 4

To make the mincemeat, put all of the dried fruit, cherries and candied peel into a large mixing bowl. Add the suet, sugar, spices, lemon rind and juice, grated orange rind and Grand Marnier. Stir in the mincemeat thoroughly and add more liqueur if not moist.

Spoon the mixture into sterilised jars, cover and leave in a cold place for 2 days or use now to make the mince pies by mixing in the chopped pear and chopped cranberries.

To make the pastry, mix all of the ingredients, except the water, in the food processor, blending for a few seconds until it starts to gather together to form a dough, and then add enough water to make a malleable dough.

Put the mixture on to a floured board and knead lightly into a firm dough. Add a little more water if the mixture is too dry and then wrap it in clingfilm (plastic wrap) and chill for 30 minutes.

Roll the dough out on to a floured board, quarter of the dough at a time, and cut with a pastry cutter into 48 × 7cm/2³/₄ inch circles (for the bases) and 48 × 5cm/2 inch circles (for the lids). Add little drops of extra water if the dough becomes too dry and crumbly when being rolled out. Grease and flour 48 non-stick patty tins and line with circles of baking parchment (wax paper). Line the prepared tins with the larger pastry circles.

Fill the pastry with a large teaspoon of mincemeat and cover with the lids. Sprinkle with caster (superfine) sugar and cinnamon and bake for 25 minutes until golden.

Leave the mince pies to cool slightly before easing them out of the tins and on to wire racks. Store in an airtight container until needed. Warm through before serving and dust with sifted icing (confectioners') sugar.

To make the custard, mix the egg yolks, sugar, cornflour (cornstarch) and ginger syrup in a large mixing bowl. Warm the milk in a non-stick saucepan and then gradually stir into the bowl of eggs. Transfer the mixture back to the saucepan and cook very gently over a low heat, stirring most of the time, until you have a thick and smooth custard. Add the ginger wine. Remove from the heat just as it reaches boiling point – do not boil. Pour into a clean bowl and stir from time to time, as it cools slightly.

Serve in two warm sauceboats with the mince pies or Christmas pudding.

Honey and Ginger Baked Pears with Sherry Ice-cream

This is a lovely wintry combination of ginger and alcohol, which is perfect with pears. The contrast of cold ice-cream with hot pears is sublime.

Serves 6–8

ICE-CREAM
5 large free-range egg yolks
100g/3¹/₂ oz/¹/₂ cup of caster (superfine) sugar
2 teaspoons of ground ginger
4 tablespoons of ginger ale
500ml/16fl oz/2 cups of soya cream
70g/2¹/₂ oz/¹/₄ cup of stem ginger, finely chopped
4 tablespoons of pale dry sherry

PEARS
6 almost ripe pears, peeled, quartered and cored
Juice of 1 lemon
1 rounded tablespoon of caster (superfine) sugar
1 heaped teaspoon of ground ginger
55g/2oz/¹/₄ cup of (DF) margarine
3 tablespoons of honey
4 tablespoons of ginger ale

Make the ice-cream first. Beat the egg yolks with the sugar, ginger and ginger ale in a food processor until pale and creamy. Transfer the mixture to a non-stick saucepan and blend in the soya cream and stem ginger.

Cook the custard over very low heat until it comes to the boil, stirring most of the time to make sure it doesn't go lumpy or curdle. As soon as it starts to boil, remove it from the heat.

Stir in the sherry. Leave the mixture to cool down, stirring frequently until it is cold.

As soon as the ice-cream maker is ready churn the custard until it is frozen. Scrape the mixture into a sealable container and freeze for a few hours or until needed (this ice-cream is soft scoop and should be served directly from the freezer).

Put the prepared pears and lemon juice into a large frying pan with the sugar, ground ginger, margarine, honey and ginger ale.

Bring the pears to the boil over medium heat and simmer for about 20 minutes, or until the pears are just soft and slightly glazed and the syrup is thick.

Serve the hot pears with the syrup on individual plates, accompanied by a large scoop of the sherry ice-cream.

Warm Butterscotch Pear Cake

Serve the cake warm with (DF) vanilla ice-cream or your choice of (DF) natural or vanilla yogurt. You can also successfully make this recipe with sweet dessert apples.

Serves 12

CAKE

2 large, just-ripe pears, peeled, quartered, cored and thinly sliced into the juice of 1 lemon
200g/7oz/1 cup less 2 tablespoons of (DF) margarine
170g/6oz/generous ¾ cup of caster (superfine) sugar
2 large free-range eggs
130g/4½oz/generous ¾ cup of rice flour
100g/3½oz/⅔ cup of maize flour
A pinch of salt
3 teaspoons of (GF) baking powder
1 heaped teaspoon of ground ginger
1 teaspoon of freshly grated nutmeg
140ml/5fl oz/⅔ cup of dry ginger ale
Finely grated zest of 1 lemon
55g/2oz/⅔ cup of ground almonds

TOPPING

55g/2oz/¼ cup of (DF) margarine
115g/4oz/½ cup plus 1 tablespoon of muscovado sugar
Few drops of Madagascan vanilla extract
100g/3½oz/1 cup of flaked almonds
Icing (confectioners') sugar to dust

Grease and line with baking parchment (wax paper) a 25cm/10 inch loose-bottomed, spring-form, round cake tin

Preheat the oven to 180°C/350°F/Gas mark 4.

Ensure the pears are prepared before beginning the cake. In a food processor, cream together the margarine and caster (superfine) sugar until pale and fluffy, then beat in the eggs. Sift together the flours with the salt, baking powder, ginger and nutmeg and briefly blend into the egg mixture. Quickly add the ginger ale, lemon zest and ground almonds, and process for a moment only. Remove the blade of the food processor and fold in half the pears in the juice.
Spoon half the cake mixture into the prepared tin and gently smooth over.
Cover the sponge with all the remaining pears and juice. Cover the pears with the remaining sponge mixture and smooth over.
Bake the cake for 40 minutes, or until golden and fairly firm.
Meanwhile, put the margarine and sugar together in a pan over medium heat and cook gently until the sugar dissolves, about 3–4 minutes will be enough. Bring it to the boil and then add the vanilla and flaked almonds. Remove from the heat and stir the mixture.
Take the cake out of the oven and spread the almond mixture over the top of the cake.
Return the cake to the oven for about 15–20 minutes, or until the topping is sticky and the sponge is firm.

Leave the cake in the tin to cool for at least 40 minutes, then carefully remove the cake from the tin and peel off the lining paper.

Place the cake on a plate and dust with sieved icing (confectioners') sugar. Serve it just warm with ice-cream or yogurt.

Little Toffee Apple Puddings

Give in to temptation and enjoy the glories of English apples baked with a hint of spices and lemon rind. I do not use cooking apples because they are too tart, so treat yourself to an old fashioned eating apple instead.

Serves 6

APPLES IN CARAMEL

2 medium dessert apples, peeled, quartered, cored, finely sliced horizontally and soaked in the juice of 1 lemon

115g/4oz/¹/₂ cup plus 1 tablespoon of caster (superfine) sugar

200ml/7fl oz/³/₄ of water

60ml/2fl oz/¹/₄ cup of dry cider

55g/2oz/¹/₄ cup of dark muscovado sugar

30g/1oz/2 tablespoons of (DF) margarine

SPONGE

A pinch of salt

130g/4¹/₂oz/generous ³/₄ cup of rice flour

130g/4¹/₂oz/generous ³/₄ cup of maize flour

2 teaspoons of (GF) baking powder

55g/2oz/4 tablespoons of light brown sugar

1 teaspoon of ground cinnamon

1 teaspoon of ground ginger

¹/₂ teaspoon of ground cloves

¹/₂ teaspoon of allspice

2 tablespoons of runny honey

1 large free-range egg

140ml/5fl oz/²/₃ cup of dry cider

125ml/4fl oz/¹/₂ cup of vegetable or sunflower oil

Grated zest of 1 lemon

Lightly oil 6 standard ovenproof ramekins and then place on a baking tray

---

Preheat the oven to 180°C/350°F/Gas mark 4.

Make sure you have the apples and lemon juice ready for the recipe.
Place the caster (superfine) sugar and water in a saucepan over medium heat and stir gently until the sugar has dissolved. Increase the heat to high and bring to the boil. Let the sugar syrup caramelize into pale golden brown colour but remove the caramel from the heat as soon as it starts to get dark or it will taste bitter. Immediately pour in the cider and beware of spluttering caramel. Set aside while you cook the apples.
Heat the muscovado sugar and margarine in a saucepan until they melt and dissolve together. Add the apples and cook over medium heat until the apples are nearly soft and coated with the sauce. As soon as most of the sauce has evaporated, stir in all the cider caramel.
Divide the mixture between the 6 prepared ramekins, then set them aside while you prepare the sponge.

Sift the dry ingredients and spices into a large bowl. In another bowl, mix the honey, egg, cider, oil and lemon zest. Stir the wet mixture into the dry mixture and immediately spoon it on to the caramelized apples in each ramekin. Gently smooth over the top and bake in the oven for 25–30 minutes, or until the sponge is golden and firm.

Let the sponges cool just enough for you to be able to hold the ramekins in a dry cloth. Ease the sponge away from the sides of the dish with a sharp knife, then turn each one on to a warm plate and serve immediately with (DF) vanilla ice-cream or (DF) yogurt.

Baked Ginger Pudding and Marsala Ice-cream

This reminds me of the school holidays when we used to have something very like this as a treat, but unfortunately not with the addition of Marsala!

Serves 6

ICE-CREAM
4 large free-range egg yolks
1 teaspoon of (GF) cornflour (cornstarch)
85g/3oz/6 tablespoons of caster (superfine) sugar
1/4 teaspoon of ground cinnamon
500ml/16fl oz/2 cups of soya cream
90ml/3fl oz/1/3 cup of Marsala

PUDDING
100g/3 1/2oz/2/3 cup of rice flour
2 teaspoons of ground cinnamon
1 teaspoon of ground ginger
A pinch of ground cloves
Freshly grated nutmeg
1 teaspoon of bicarbonate of soda (baking soda)

100g/3 1/2oz/1/2 cup of soft dark brown sugar
1 large free-range egg
140ml/5fl oz/2/3 cup of Marsala
75g/3oz/1/4 cup of black treacle (molasses)
55g/2oz/1/4 cup of (DF) margarine, melted
Zest of 1 large orange
100g/3 1/2oz/3/4 cup of stem ginger, drained and chopped or sugar-coated ginger pieces
85g/3oz/1/2 cup of plump raisins
Extra grated nutmeg and ground cinnamon for decoration

A large, terrine tin or loaf tin, lined with baking parchment (wax paper)

Preheat the oven to 180°C/350°F/Gas mark 4

Make the ice-cream first. Whisk the egg yolks with the cornflour (cornstarch) and caster sugar. Add the cinnamon and cream and cook in a non-stick saucepan over low heat until it reaches boiling point. Do not let it boil. Remove the pan from the heat and quickly stir in the Marsala. Allow the mixture to cool, stirring it occasionally to prevent a skin forming.

Transfer the mixture to the ice-cream maker and churn until frozen. This will probably take about 20 minutes.

Scrape the ice-cream into a sealable container and freeze for 2–4 hours before serving with the pudding.

Make the pudding. Sieve the flour into a bowl along with the spices, bicarbonate of soda (baking soda) and sugar. Beat in the egg, followed by the Marsala, treacle, melted margarine and orange zest. Stir in the ginger and raisins.

Pour the mixture into the prepared tin and bake for 35 minutes. Have the ice-cream at room temperature 10 minutes before serving.

Turn the cake out of the tin and peel off the baking parchment (wax paper). Cut the cake into thick slices, place a slice on each plate with a scoop of ice-cream and sprinkle with a little grated nutmeg and ground cinnamon.

CHAPTER 3

Chilled Puddings

Fruits of every colour and shape imaginable are available during the summer, making it possible to combine different varieties and textures, which can provide astonishingly delicious results.

Berries are so versatile and can now be bought (although at huge expense) all year round. But nothing beats freshly picked organic seasonal fruit anywhere in the world, when it is full of goodness, nourishing and refreshing.

Ice-creams and sorbets are now no longer an endurance test of endless patience and interminable stirring. Marvellous gelati/ice-cream makers exist with a built in freezer which produce refreshing and exotic puddings in 20 minutes. There is no need to miss out any more because all the ice-creams you see in the supermarket are made with dairy. You can now create exactly the same sort of ices at home in your machine. Using some alternative ingredients, you can produce spectacular ices, so go for it and experiment!

French Apple Tart

A classic piece of French pâtisserie, which I have tried to make quicker in case time is short between getting home from work and friends coming to dinner.

Serves 10

140g/5oz/1 cup of rice flour
140g/5oz/1 cup of maize flour
140g/5oz/²/₃ cup of (DF) margarine
55g/2oz/4 tablespoons of caster (superfine) sugar
A pinch of salt
1 large free-range egg
500ml/16fl oz/2 cups of pure and sweetened

ready-made apple purée
3 large sweet dessert apples, peeled, quartered, cored
and left in the juice of ¹/₂ a small lemon
115g/4oz/¹/₃ cup of apricot jam (jelly)

Grease and flour a fluted loose-bottomed 32cm/12¹/₂
inch tart tin

Preheat the oven to 200°C/400°F/Gas mark 6

Combine the flours, margarine, sugar, salt and egg together in a food processor with 2 tablespoons of cold water. Process until it forms a ball of dough.
Put the pastry into the middle of the prepared tin and gently flatten it with floured hands, gently pushing the pastry out until it reaches the sides and then up the fluted sides to the top. Trim the pastry with a knife and discard the trimmings.
Pour the apple purée into the pastry and smooth over. Slice the apple quarters horizontally into wafer thin slices and arrange in overlapping circles in the tart.
Bake the tart for 45 minutes, or until the apples are browned and tender. Keep the tart in the tin whilst it cools down.
Heat the apricot jam (jelly) in a small bowl in the microwave and spread all over the apples.
Once the tart is cold, remove it carefully from the tin and serve on a plate.
This is delicious with (DF) vanilla ice-cream, if you can not eat crème fraiche.

Vacherin aux Marrons

If you have had enough of strawberries then this recipe is delicious made with raspberries in the summer or poached, canned pears in the winter.

Serves 8–12

4 large free-range egg whites

225g/8oz/1 cup of caster sugar

1 teaspoon of Madagascan vanilla extract

225g/8oz/2 cups of chopped walnuts

425g/15oz of canned unsweetened chestnut purée

55g/2oz/½ cup of icing (confectioners') sugar, sifted

2 tablespoons of dark rum

2 tablespoons of soya cream, or sufficient to make a spreadable purée

500g/17oz/3½ cups fresh strawberries, washed, hulled and left to dry

30g/1oz (GF and DF) continental dark chocolate, coarsely grated

Extra icing (confectioners') sugar sifted, to decorate

Draw around 2 dinner plates on 2 sheets of baking parchment (wax paper) and place each sheet on a non-stick baking tray.

Preheat the oven to 180°C/350°F/Gas mark 4

Whisk the egg whites until they stand in stiff peaks. Whisk in the sugar, a little at a time, until thick and glossy. Fold in the vanilla and nuts using a metal spoon.

Lightly spread the mixture over both of the prepared circles of paper.

Bake the meringues in the oven for about 35–45 minutes, or until lightly coloured on top and set inside (unless you are very lucky and have two ovens, I usually swap their positions around at half time, so that they are evenly cooked).

Meanwhile, beat the chestnut purée with the icing (confectioners') sugar, rum and soya cream until it reaches a spreadable consistency.

Slice up the strawberries.

As soon as the vacherin is cold, carefully peel off the paper and place one vacherin on to a serving plate. Spread all the chestnut purée on the top of the base and then cover with the strawberries. Cover with the remaining vacherin and decorate the top with the grated chocolate and sifted icing (confectioners') sugar.

Orange Mousse with Almonds

This is more of an exotic orange custard than a mousse. It is delicious served in little ramekins and enjoyed with tiny almond cookies.

Serves 4–6

115g/4oz/¹⁄₂ cup plus 1 tablespoon caster (superfine) sugar

4 large free-range egg yolks

1 whole free-range egg

3 tablespoons of pale dry sherry

2 heaped tablespoons of ground almonds

Zest from 1 large or 2 small oranges

300ml/10fl oz/1¹⁄₄ cups of freshly squeezed orange juice

11.7g/¹⁄₂oz sachet (US 1 tablespoon) of powdered gelatine, dissolved in 100ml/3fl oz/¹⁄₃ cup of boiling water

1 tablespoon of toasted almond slivers

Beat the sugar, egg yolks and whole egg in a food processor until pale and creamy. Briefly blend in the sherry, ground almonds and orange zest. Transfer the mixture to a large bowl.

Microwave the orange juice until boiling and frothy and then whisk it into the egg mixture at full speed on an electric mixer. Pour in the prepared gelatine, whisking all the time to distribute it evenly.

Pour the mixture into a small soufflé dish or 4–6 ramekins. Leave the mousse to set in the freezer for about 40 minutes, then transfer to the refrigerator for at least 3 hours or until firm. Decorate the mousse with the almond slivers and serve chilled.

Strawberry Tarts with Rose Zabaglione

Raspberries are just as delicious as strawberries in these lovely little tarts and very ripe and juicy blackberries in the autumn too. You can always use orange blossom water instead of rosewater for the blackberries.

Makes 16 small or 8 large tarts

PASTRY

200g/7oz/scant 1½ cups of The Stamp Collection (WF) flour
55g/2oz/½ cup of icing (confectioners') sugar
A pinch of salt
100g/3½oz/7 tablespoons of (DF) margarine
1 large free-range egg

variegated lemon balm, to decorate
12–16 greased and floured bun tin trays, lined with baking parchment (wax paper) circles

FILLING

750g/1lb 10oz/5½ cups of fresh strawberries, hulled and wiped clean
340g/12oz/1 generous cup of redcurrant jelly to glaze the fruit

ROSE ZABAGLIONE

4 large free-range egg yolks
70g/2½oz/⅓ cup of caster (superfine) sugar
75ml/2½ fl oz/¼ cup of white rum
3 tablespoons of rosewater

Preheat the oven to 180°C/350°F/Gas mark 4

Make the pastry by putting all the pastry ingredients, except the egg, together in the food processor and mixing until it resembles breadcrumbs. Now add the egg and pulse until the dough comes together into a ball.

Cut the pastry in half and roll out each half on a floured surface with a floured rolling pin. Cut out 12–16 circles with a 8½ cm/3¼ inch cutter and line each prepared bun tin with the pastry. Place a circle of baking parchment (wax paper) in each one and secure with some baking beans. Bake blind in the oven for 20 minutes, or until the pastry is golden and crispy.

Remove the tarts from the oven to cool but leave them in the tins. Once they are nearly cold, transfer them to a wire rack.

Cut the strawberries into quarters in order to keep them to an even size and pile plenty of the fruit into each tart.

Use as much or as little jelly as you like to glaze the fruit. Melt the jelly in a small bowl in the microwave and brush each tart with the warm jelly.

Make the zabaglione just before serving. Fill a saucepan a third of the way up with water and bring to the boil. Put the egg yolks and sugar into a large heatproof bowl and beat together with an electric whisk.

Add the rum and rosewater. Place the bowl over the saucepan of simmering water and whisk on high speed until very thick. Serve immediately.

Place a tart on each plate surrounded by a pool of the zabaglione and decorate with a sprig of variegated lemon balm.

Pineapple Pavlova with Kiwi Sauce

Over the years, I have seen Pavlovas filled with masses of different fruits and creams and they have all been delicious. This one, however, is my favourite because there is a wonderful contrast between the tart kiwi sauce and the sweet, crunchy and marshmallowy meringue.

Serves 8

PAVLOVA
285g/10oz/1 ½ cups of caster (superfine) sugar
1 rounded teaspoon of (GF) cornflour (cornstarch)
5 large free-range egg whites
1 teaspoon of cider or white wine vinegar

FILLING
8 ripe kiwi fruit, peeled, trimmed and quartered
Caster (superfine) sugar to taste

White rum to taste
(DF) vanilla ice-cream
1 medium pineapple, peeled, trimmed, core removed
 and the flesh cut into bite-sized cubes

A baking tray lined with a sheet of non-stick (wax)
 paper
Draw a circle on the baking parchment (wax paper),
 around a 23cm/9 inch plate

Preheat the oven to 150°C/300°F/Gas mark 2

Sift the caster (superfine) sugar and cornflour (cornstarch) together into a bowl and set aside. Whisk the egg whites in a large bowl until they form stiff peaks, then fold in the vinegar. Whisk in 50g/2oz/¼ cup of the sugar mixture then, using a metal spoon, fold in the remainder a quarter at a time. Try to let in as much air as possible.

Gently spread the meringue over the circle of paper. Use the back of the spoon to swirl out an indentation in the centre of the meringue and build up the edges higher than the middle. Use a fork to create some peaks around the edge.

Cook the Pavlova in the oven for about 25 minutes, or until well risen and a light pinkish-brown. Reduce the heat to 140°C/275°F/Gas mark 1 and cook for another 50 minutes. Turn off the heat but do not open the door. Leave the Pavlova for 2–6 hours inside the oven.

Remove the meringue from the oven and carefully peel away the baking parchment (wax paper). Place the meringue on a serving dish.

Very briefly purée the kiwi fruit in a food processor, but do not use a blender as this results in a discoloured sauce. Add enough sugar to taste and stir in enough rum to the sauce to make it a perfect pouring consistency. Sieve the sauce to remove the pips and then transfer it to a serving jug.

Fill the pavlova with the ice-cream, then cover with the pineapple and serve immediately with the accompanying sauce.

Clementine and Orange Jelly

English jelly dates back to the 14th century, and became grander and more elaborate over the centuries. Blancmanges evolved and beautiful gleaming copper and china jelly moulds of every shape and size hung in kitchens until the 1960s, when sadly we 'progressed' to mass-produced jellies.

Serves 4

The juice of 6 large juicy oranges

60ml/2fl oz/¼ cup of Cointreau, orange liqueur (or clementine juice for children)

11.7g/½oz sachet (US 1 tablespoon) of powdered gelatine dissolved according to instructions on packet

310g/11½oz/1½ cups of fresh, seedless clementines, peeled, pith removed and segments chopped (canned fruit is fine, just drain the juices)

A few spare segments of clementines and fresh mint to decorate

Mix the orange juice with the Cointreau in a bowl and vigorously stir in the gelatine as soon as it has dissolved. Add the chopped clementines and chill for 1 hour, before giving it a thoroughly good stir to distribute the clementines more evenly.

Pour the jelly into glasses or individual tin moulds and chill for 4 hours, or until set.

When the jellies are set, decorate them in the glasses with spare clementines and fresh mint leaves. Alternatively, dip the moulds into boiling water for a few seconds and turn out the jellies on to small plates and decorate around the jelly.

For children, omit the liqueur and mint leaves and make the jellies in pretty paper cups.

Chocolate Sorbet

A blissfully sinful sorbet, not remotely slimming, but quite delicious with cookies or the Almond Petit Fours recipe on page 96.

Serves 6

200g/7oz/1 cup of caster (superfine) sugar
140g/5oz of (GF& DF) continental dark chocolate
A pinch of salt
1 teaspoon of ground cinnamon
600ml/22fl oz/2³/₄ cups of water
1 tablespoon of rum

90ml/3fl oz/¹/₃ cup of fresh strong black coffee
100g/3¹/₂oz/³/₄ cup of plump raisins

Fresh sprigs of rosemary and seasonal berries or fruits
  for decoration

Simmer all the ingredients – except the rum, coffee and the raisins – in a heavy-bottomed pan and bring to the boil. Continue to cook for 5 minutes and then strain into a bowl.

Add the rum, coffee and raisins, and allow to cool.

Churn and freeze the sorbet in an ice-cream maker for 20 minutes, or until frozen but manageable. Scrape into a sealable container and freeze until needed.

Serve the sorbet straight from the freezer.

A couple of scoops on a plate with some fresh rosemary leaves and a little display of seasonal fresh fruit, looks great.

Mango Passion Mousse

This feather light mousse, which is covered with glistening pools of passion fruit, is ideal for a large buffet or party at any time of the year.

Serves 12–14

Seeds from 10 cardamom pods

6 large free-range egg yolks

2 tablespoons of caster (superfine) sugar

240ml/8fl oz/1 cup of soya cream

200ml/7fl oz/3/4 cup of coconut cream

3 tablespoons of Cointreau

2 medium (approximately 600g/1lb 5oz each) ripe mangoes, peeled and the flesh sliced off the stone and chopped roughly

1 freshly squeezed orange

Juice of 1 lemon

1 1/2 sachets (16g/3/4oz/US 1 1/2 tablespoons) powdered gelatine, dissolved in 60ml/2fl oz/1/4 cup of boiling water and stirred until dissolved

3 large free-range egg whites

5 large ripe passion fruit, halved and seeds and juices scooped out and used for decoration

Put the cardamom seeds into a non-stick saucepan with the egg yolks and sugar and beat with a wooden spoon.

Gradually add the soya cream, then the coconut cream. Cook the mixture over a low heat until it thickens and comes almost to boiling point, stirring constantly. Remove from the heat and continue to stir.

Add the Cointreau and leave the custard to cool in a clean bowl, stirring occasionally.

Purée the mango and fruit juices together in a food processor until smooth, then stir the purée into the custard.

As soon as the mixture is a little cooler, stir in the dissolved gelatine. Set aside until the mixture is cold.

Whisk the egg whites in a separate bowl until they form stiff peaks. Add a little of the custard to the whisked egg whites and fold in gently. Quickly fold the egg white mixture into the remaining custard using a metal spoon and transfer to a large glass serving bowl. Level off the top and freeze for 40 minutes, to help it set quickly.

Remove the mousse from the freezer and cover with clingfilm (plastic wrap). Chill in the refrigerator for 4 hours or until it is firm and set.

Decorate the mousse by sprinkling spoonfuls of passion fruit over the surface. Serve the mousse chilled.

Banana and Pecan Ice-cream with Damson Coulis

Autumn starts when the damsons appear, heralding the rich colours of the season. This luscious purple fruit is a dramatic contrast to the pale ice-cream it is served with. A variation of this dish can be made at any time of year by using the out-of-season sauce.

Serves 8–12

DAMSON COULIS

500g/17oz/4 cups of damsons, stalks and any bad
  patches removed
4 or more tablespoons of caster (superfine) sugar
  (increase to suit taste)
4 tablespoons of damson gin, sloe gin or white rum
Water and more of the chosen spirit to correct the
  consistency if necessary

QUICK OUT-OF-SEASON SAUCE

450g/16oz jar of forest fruits or stoned (pitted) black
  cherries in liqueur or brandy
or
450g/16oz can of soft red fruits or black cherries in
  natural juices

ICE-CREAM

5 large free-range egg yolks
2 teaspoons of (GF) cornflour (cornstarch)
2 tablespoons of caster (superfine) sugar
500ml/16fl oz/2 cups of soya cream
2 teaspoons of mixed spice (pie spice)
100g/3½oz/¾ cup of chopped pecans
4 tablespoons of pure maple syrup
2 tablespoons of brandy
4 large, ripe, mashed bananas in the juice of ½ a
  lemon

Make the damson coulis by gently cooking the fruit, sugar and gin in a pan, over medium heat, until the fruit is soft. Add water if the damsons start to stick, but only add a little at a time, otherwise the sauce will be too runny.

Let the fruit get cold, then pass the fruit and its liquid through a sieve into a bowl. Discard the fruit skins and stones. Add more sugar, water or additional alcohol to taste, and to achieve the perfect consistency.

Transfer the coulis to a serving jug and chill until needed.

If damsons are unavailable, use the fruits suggested for the out-of-season sauce and liquidize them in their juices.

Sieve the sauce to remove any pips or skins, place in a serving jug and chill until needed.

To make the ice-cream, beat the egg yolks with the cornflour (cornstarch) and sugar in a non-stick saucepan. Gradually incorporate the soya cream, mixed spice (pie spice) and pecans.

Stir the custard over low heat until it comes to the boil, then remove from the heat and stir in the maple syrup and brandy.

Let the mixture cool slightly and then stir in the mashed bananas and lemon juice.

Once the mixture is cool, and your ice-cream maker is ready, churn the ice-cream for about 20 minutes or until it is frozen.

Scrape out the ice-cream and store in an airtight container in the freezer until needed.

Serve the ice-cream in a large scoop with the damson or fruit coulis poured all around it.

Christmas Pudding Ice-cream

Here is an ideal way of using up Christmas pudding leftovers and getting away with serving it as a party piece! Decorate it as ostentatiously as you like to suit the occasion. We will definitely be having this on New Year's Eve.

Serves 6

6 heaped tablespoons of leftover (GF& DF) Christmas pudding

8 small free-range egg yolks

1 tablespoon of (GF) cornflour (cornstarch)

2 heaped tablespoons of caster (superfine) sugar

1 teaspoon of Madagascan pure vanilla extract

300ml/10fl oz/1¼ cups of soya milk

225ml/7½ fl oz/generous ¾ cup of soya cream

200ml/7fl oz/¾ cup of coconut cream

3 tablespoons of rum

Clingfilm (plastic wrap)

A sprig of holly for decoration

Line a pudding basin with clingfilm (plastic wrap). Crumble up the leftover Christmas pudding and put it into a large bowl. Mix the eggs in a separate bowl with the cornflour (cornstarch), sugar and vanilla extract. Gradually add the milk until it is all well blended. Transfer the mixture to a non-stick saucepan and cook slowly, stirring often, until it becomes very thick.

Let the custard come to the boil, then remove from the heat and stir in the soya cream, coconut cream and finally the rum. Pass the custard through a fine sieve into the bowl of Christmas pudding.

Gently mix it all together, then allow the mixture to cool.

When the ice-cream maker is ready, churn the custard and Christmas pudding mixture until frozen but still soft enough to scrape out of the bowl.

Spoon the ice-cream into the lined basin, smooth over and seal with the clingfilm (plastic wrap). Freeze for 4 hours or more.

Remove the clingfilm (plastic wrap) from the pudding and turn out on to a plate. Peel off the remaining clingfilm (plastic wrap), put a sprig of holly on top and serve immediately.

Sherry Cake and Baked Figs

A splash of Sherry or Marsala transforms this cake into an exciting delicacy. Both these fortified wines bring the full taste sensation of sun-baked, ripe Mediterranean figs bursting in your mouth as you bite into them.

Serves 6

CAKE

70g/2½oz/½ cup of potato flour

100g/3½oz/⅔ cup of maize flour

100g/3½oz/⅔ cup of rice flour

2 teaspoons of (GF) baking powder

A pinch of salt

225ml/7½ fl oz/generous ¾ cup of light sunflower oil

225g/8oz/1 generous cup of caster (superfine) sugar

4 large free-range eggs

130g/4½oz/1½ cups of ground almonds

Grated zest of 1 lemon

125ml/4fl oz/½ cup of aged Amontillado dry sherry

Icing (confectioners') sugar to decorate

FIGS

12 ripe, but firm, figs

Juice of 1 large orange

¾ teaspoon of pure Madagascan vanilla extract

1 teaspoon of mixed spice (pie spice)

A little grated nutmeg

3 tablespoons of Marsala

3 tablespoons of runny honey

Grease a non-stick 20cm/8inch cake tin and dust with extra flour

Preheat the oven to 180°C/350°F/Gas mark 4

Sift the flours, baking powder and salt into a large bowl. In another bowl, whisk the oil with the sugar and beat in the eggs, one at a time, until thick and creamy.

Gently fold the egg mixture into the flours. Carefully add the almonds, lemon zest and sherry, and spoon the cake mixture into the prepared tin.

Bake for 1 hour, or until an inserted skewer comes out clean.

Allow the cake to cool, then turn out on to a wire rack and leave until cold.

Wash the figs and place them in an ovenproof dish with the orange juice, vanilla, spices and Marsala. Pour the honey over the figs and bake for 35 minutes or until soft and glazed.

Put the cake on a plate and sprinkle it with sieved icing (confectioners') sugar. Serve the figs warm or cold with the cake.

Lemon Tart

This should be baked the day before and kept in the refrigerator, making it an an ideal pudding if you are going to be rushed off your feet on the day of your party.

Serves 8

PASTRY
85g/3oz/6 tablespoons of (DF) margarine
45g/1½oz/3 tablespoons of caster (superfine) sugar
Grated zest of 1 lemon
1 large free-range egg
55g/2oz/scant ½ cup of rice flour
55g/2oz/scant ½ cup of maize flour

FILLING
3 large free-range eggs
3 large free-range egg yolks
180ml/6½ fl oz/generous ⅔ cup of lemon juice

Zest of 1 lemon
200g/7oz/1 cup of caster (superfine) sugar
55g/2oz/¼ cup of (DF) margarine
2 tablespoons of caster (superfine) sugar for sprinkling
8 wafer thin slices of lemon, halved
Extra icing (confectioners') sugar for decoration

Grease and flour a 24cm/9½ inch loose-bottomed tart tin
Baking parchment (wax paper) and ceramic baking beans

Preheat the oven to 200°C/400°F/Gas mark 6

Briefly mix the margarine, sugar and grated lemon zest in a food processor. Add the egg and beat for a moment or two. Mix in the flours until it comes together into a dough. Shape the pastry into a ball, wrap in clingfilm (plastic wrap) and chill for 1 hour.

Roll out the dough on a floured surface to the shape of the tin. Transfer the pastry to the tin and press into the tin with floured fingers. Trim the edges and prick all over the base of the pastry with a fork.

Line the pastry with the baking parchment (wax paper), cover with ceramic beans and bake for 15 minutes. Carefully remove the ceramic beans and baking parchment (wax paper) and cook the pastry in the oven for a further 5 minutes. Set aside to cool.

Now make the filling in a food processor. Beat the 3 whole eggs with the 3 extra yolks, lemon juice and zest, and sugar. Transfer to a non-stick saucepan and cook gently over medium heat. Stir frequently and do not allow it to boil. When the mixture is thick, remove from the heat, add the margarine and stir until it has melted.

Pour the filling into the pastry shell and chill in the refrigerator for 12 hours.

A couple of hours before serving the lemon tart, turn the grill on to very hot. Sprinkle the extra sugar over the lemon filling and decorate with the lemon slices. Grill for about 6–8 minutes until the tart is browned but not scorched.

Chill the tart again until needed. To serve, slide the base off the tin on to a serving dish and decorate the tart with a sprinkling of extra sifted icing (confectioners') sugar.

Chocolate Profiteroles

Once you can make profiteroles, all sorts of alternatives can be dreamt up. In this recipe the profiteroles are filled with coffee crème patissière and covered in coffee icing, but you could also fill them with (DF) ice-cream and serve with a fruit sauce.

Serves 6 (4 each)

PROFITEROLES

55g/2oz/¼ cup of (DF) margarine
70g/2½oz/½ cup of rice flour
2 large free-range eggs
200g/7oz/generous cup (WF and DF) plain chocolate
4 tablespoons of freshly brewed espresso coffee
20g/¾oz/1½ tablespoons of (DF) margarine

CRÈME PATISSIÈRE

450ml/15fl oz/1¾ cups of soya milk
55g/2oz/scant ¼ cup of caster (superfine) sugar
55g/2oz/⅓ cup of (GF) cornflour (cornstarch)
2 large free-range egg yolks
4 tablespoons of very strong espresso coffee

Baking parchment (wax paper)

Preheat the oven to 220°C/425°F/Gas mark 7

Mix all the ingredients for the crème patissière in a food processor until smooth, then transfer to a non-stick saucepan.

Cook over medium heat until the custard is thick. Bring to the boil and remove from the heat immediately. Allow the custard to cool slightly, then transfer to a bowl. Cover with baking parchment (wax paper) to prevent a skin forming and chill for 1 hour.

If it is then too firm to spoon or pipe into the profiteroles, add a little more coffee and beat until smooth and manageable.

Make the profiteroles. Heat a pan containing 125ml/4fl oz/½ cup of water and the 55g/2oz/¼ cup of margarine until boiling. Remove from the heat and tip all the flour into the water. Beat vigorously with a wooden spoon until the mixture leaves the sides of the pan. Add one egg at a time, beating until the dough is smooth and shiny.

Drop 24 teaspoons of dough on to a non-stick baking tray, keeping them about 5cm/2 inches apart. Bake for 25–30 minutes, or until puffy and golden. (Try not to open the oven door until they are ready or they might sink!)

When the profiteroles are ready, remove them from the oven and very quickly pierce them with a sharp knife around the middle. This allows the steam to escape and prevents them from going soggy. Transfer them to a wire rack to cool.

Meanwhile, place the chocolate in a bowl with the coffee and the 20g/¾oz/1½ tablespoons of margarine and melt in the microwave. When melted, stir until smooth and keep to one side.

Slice each cold profiterole across and spoon or pipe in the filling. Close the profiterole and place on a serving plate.

It is traditional to build up the profiteroles into a pyramid shape but they can be arranged however you like. Pour the warm sauce over the tops and serve. The profiteroles can be kept chilled until needed, but serve them on the day of making.

Elderflower and Gooseberry Cream

Lush, ripe gooseberries capture the essence of the best of British soft summer fruit. Abundant in August, gooseberries are easy to freeze and make lovely sauces, soufflés and pies.

Serves 8

ELDERFLOWER CREAM

11.7g/¹/₂oz sachet (US 1 tablespoon) of powdered gelatine dissolved in 60ml/2fl oz/¹/₄ cup of boiling water

100ml/3¹/₂fl oz/7 tablespoons of elderflower and lemon cordial

550g/1lb 3oz/4 cups of trimmed, ripe dessert gooseberries

2 tablespoons of caster (superfine) sugar

2 large free-range eggs, separated

200ml/7fl oz/³/₄ cup of coconut cream

240ml/8fl oz/1 cup of soya cream

Fresh mint leaves and sifted icing (confectioners') sugar to decorate

Mix the dissolved gelatine with the elderflower cordial.

Cook the gooseberries with the sugar and a tiny amount of water, just enough so that the fruit will not stick to the pan. When the fruit is bursting and soft, remove from the heat.

When the fruit is nearly cold, place in the food processor and beat to a thick purée. Sieve the purée into a bowl in order to remove all the pips.

Stir the egg yolks and gelatine into the fruit purée and mix thoroughly. Mix in the coconut cream and soya cream.

In another bowl, whisk the egg whites until stiff and then fold into the purée using a metal spoon.

Fill a large pretty bowl or dish with the elderflower and gooseberry cream and leave it to chill in the in the freezer for about 30–40 minutes.

Once it is starting to set, cover the dish with clingfilm (plastic wrap) and chill it for at least 4 more hours in the refrigerator.

Once the elderflower cream is completely set, decorate it with little sprigs of fresh mint.

At the last moment dust the elderflower and gooseberry cream with sifted icing (confectioners') sugar and serve chilled with some crunchy (GF& DF) cookies.

Chocolate and Ginger Biscuit Cake

This delicious cake is quick and easy to make. Make sure you have a secret supply of (GF, WF and DF) ginger biscuits or chocolate biscuits in the cupboard, as this makes a great emergency pudding.

Serves 6

CRUST
125g/4¹/₂oz package of (GF/WF/DF) gingernut cookies
55g/2oz/¹/₄ cup of (DF) margarine, melted
55g/2oz/scant ¹/₄ cup of caster (superfine) sugar

FILLING
340g/12oz of (DF) dark chocolate
140g/5oz/¹/₂ cup plus 2 tablespoons of (DF) margarine

240ml/8fl oz/1 cup of soya cream
4 tablespoons of ginger wine, or the drained syrup from the stem ginger
2 large free-range eggs, separated
100g/3¹/₂oz/¹/₂cup of stem ginger in syrup, drained and finely chopped
A little (DF &GF) cocoa powder to dust

Lightly oil an ovenproof china or glass tart dish 24cm/9¹/₂ inch x 4cm/1¹/₂ inches deep.

Preheat the oven to 180°C/350°F/Gas mark 4

Make the crust by mixing the cookies with the margarine and sugar in a food processor until it resembles a loose crumbly mixture.

Press the crumb mixture into the base of the prepared dish, ensuring it is level. Bake in the oven for 10 minutes and then set aside to cool.

Once the base is cold, make the filling by melting the chocolate, margarine, soya cream, ginger wine or syrup in a bowl in the microwave until soft. Remove from the microwave and stir until smooth. Add the egg yolks to the mixture, blend in and then mix in the chopped ginger.

In a separate bowl, whisk the egg whites until they form stiff peaks and fold them gently into the chocolate mixture.

Pour the mixture on to the crust and level off. Chill for 1 hour in the freezer, before transferring to the refrigerator to set.

Cover until needed. Just before serving, dust the biscuit cake with sieved cocoa powder and serve chilled for the best results.

Redcurrant and Lime Meringue Tarts

These deliciously chewy tarts are easy to transport on picnics, or for summer parties in the garden. You can use any soft fruit you like for the recipe and in winter, mincemeat is also a delicious option.

Serves 14

PASTRY

200g/7oz/scant 1½ cups of The Stamp Collection
   (WF) flour
55g/2oz/½ cup of icing (confectioners') sugar
A pinch of salt
100g/3½oz/7 tablespoons of (DF) margarine
1 large free-range egg

FILLING

455g/1lb/2⅔ cups of redcurrants
200g/7oz/1 cup of caster (superfine) sugar

3 large free-range egg whites
A pinch of salt
Finely grated zest of 2 small limes
½ teaspoon of cream of tartar
30g/1oz/scant ¼ cup of The Stamp Collection (WF)
   flour, sifted
¼ teaspoon of (WF) baking powder
100g/3½oz/1 cup of desiccated (shredded) coconut

2 or more greased and floured bun tin trays, lined
   with baking parchment (wax paper) circles

Preheat the oven to 180°C/350°F/Gas mark 4

Make the pastry by combining all the pastry ingredients, except the egg, in the food processor until the mixture resembles breadcrumbs. Add the egg and pulse until the dough comes together into a ball.

Cut the pastry in half and roll out, one half at a time, on a floured surface with a floured rolling pin. Cut our 12 or more circles with a 8½ cm/3¼ inch cutter and line each prepared bun tin with the pastry circles.

Divide the redcurrants between the tarts, but do not over fill or they will overflow and become too sticky (if they are large fresh redcurrants then you may not need all the fruit). Sprinkle a little of the sugar over them if the fruit is very sharp.

Make the meringue by whisking the egg whites until stiff in a large bowl with the salt. Gradually beat in all the sugar, then change to a very low speed and add the zest of the limes, followed by the cream of tartar, flour and baking powder. Lastly fold in the coconut.

Place a spoonful of meringue on to each tart, keeping the meringue within the boundaries of the pastry so that it doesn't stick to the sides of the tin.

Bake in the oven for about 20–25 minutes, or until the pastry and meringue is golden brown and firm.

Leave the tarts in the tins until they are only just warm. Carefully ease them out of the tins, discard the paper circles and serve the tarts warm or cold.

Chocolate and Chestnut Pavé

This is ideal for Christmas or New Year entertaining as it is intensely rich, easy to prepare and can be made a day in advance, which is always useful when the house is full of demanding guests.

Serves 10

435g/15oz can of unsweetened chestnut purée
200ml/7fl oz/³/₄ cup of golden syrup (corn syrup)
310g/11oz/scant 2 cups of (DF) continental dark
   chocolate, finely chopped in a food processor
55g/2oz/¹/₂ cup of (DF) margarine, sliced up

225g/8oz/1 ¹/₃ cups of peeled and chopped chestnuts

A loaf/terrine tin lined with clingfilm (plastic wrap)
Sieved (DF) cocoa powder and fresh physalis fruits
   (Cape gooseberries) to decorate

Gently heat the chestnut purée in a non-stick saucepan with the syrup, stirring until smooth and well blended. Add the chopped chocolate and stir until melted and thoroughly mixed.
Remove from the heat and stir in the margarine until it has melted and blended in. Mix in the chestnuts and cool slightly. Spoon the mixture into the prepared loaf or terrine tin.
When the mixture is cold, cover it with foil and chill for 1 hour in the freezer, then another hour in the refrigerator. Leave it in the refrigerator until you are ready to serve it.
Turn out the Pavé and peel off the clingfilm (plastic wrap). Serve one slice per person on each plate and decorate with sifted cocoa powder and a couple of physalis (Cape gooseberries) with the wings peeled back for effect.

Classic Chocolate Mousse

As light as a cloud and as popular now as it was 20 years ago, this classic French mousse can not be changed because it is utterly perfect.

Serves 6

225g/8oz/1⅓ cups of (DF) dark continental chocolate
15g/½oz/1 tablespoon of (DF) margarine
1 tablespoon of Cognac or brandy

4 large free-range eggs, separated

6 standard ramekins

Break the chocolate into small pieces, place in a large bowl with 4 tablespoons of water and melt in the microwave. Stir in the margarine and Cognac and microwave very briefly. Now stir in the egg yolks.

In another bowl, whisk the egg whites until they are stiff and forming firm peaks. Now fold the egg whites into the chocolate mixture using a metal spoon. Gently spoon the mousse mixture into each ramekin and carefully level off.

Cover each mousse with clingfilm (plastic wrap) and chill them for several hours or until they are firmly set.

Remove the clingfilm (plastic wrap) and serve each ramekin on a little plate with a couple of tiny (GF& DF) cookies.

Mocha Mousse Cake

The base for this cake can also be made into delicious cookies. Dust them with extra sugar and serve with (DF) ice-cream or just with freshly brewed coffee for a special treat.

Serves 6–8

SHORTBREAD CRUST
100g/3¹/₂oz/7 tablespoons of (DF) margarine
5 tablespoons of caster (superfine) sugar
1 teaspoon of Madagascan vanilla extract
100g/3¹/₂oz/²/₃ cup of rice flour
5 tablespoons of unsweetened (DF) cocoa powder
¹/₄ teaspoon of salt
100g/3¹/₂oz/1 generous cup of ground almonds
2 tablespoons of caster (superfine) sugar
55g/2oz/¹/₄ cup of melted (DF) margarine

MOCHA MOUSSE
100g/3¹/₂oz of (DF) dark continental chocolate

4 large free-range egg yolks
100g/3¹/₂oz/¹/₂ cup of caster (superfine) sugar
140ml/5fl oz/²/₃ cup of strong freshly brewed, hot
   black coffee
11.7g/¹/₂oz sachet (US 1 tablespoon) powdered
   gelatine dissolved in 60m/¹/₂fl oz/¹/₂ cup of boiling
   water
3 large free-range egg whites

8–16 fresh coffee beans for decoration and a little
   extra (DF) cocoa powder
A lightly oiled 23cm/9-inch deep sided china or glass
   tart or flan dish

Preheat the oven to 180°C/350°F/Gas mark 4

Make the shortbread crust first. Mix together the margarine, sugar and vanilla until pale and creamy, in either a bowl or a food processor. Sift together the flour, cocoa and salt on to a plate. Add the dry ingredients to the margarine mixture and beat together until the dough forms into a ball. Wrap the dough in clingfilm (plastic wrap) and chill for 30 minutes.

On a lightly oiled surface, roll out the dough to 1.25cm/¹/₂-inch thick and slide it on to a non-stick baking tray. Bake it in the oven for 25–35 minutes, but do not let the crust blacken around the edges. (Alternatively, if you are making cookies, cut out 5cm/2 inch circles instead and transfer them to a non-stick baking tray, leaving plenty of room for them to spread. Bake the cookies for 20–25 minutes or until firm to touch. Cool on a wire rack.)

When the shortbread crust has cooled down, break it up into pieces and allow it to get cold. Process the shortbread crust briefly in a food processor until it resembles breadcrumbs. Quickly add the almonds, 2 tablespoons of caster (superfine) sugar and the melted margarine, and mix for a second or two.

Pack the mixture into the prepared dish, press down firmly and then leave to cool in the refrigerator.

Meanwhile, melt the chocolate in a large bowl in the microwave until just soft and then stir until smooth. Beat the egg yolks in a food processor with the caster (superfine) sugar until pale and smooth. Pour in the hot coffee and process again. Pour in the melted gelatine and briefly process again. Stir the coffee mixture into the bowl of chocolate until well blended.

Leave the mousse to cool in the refrigerator for 20 minutes.

Put the egg whites in a large bowl, beat until stiff and fold into the mousse mixture using a metal spoon.

Pour the mousse over the biscuit base, level off and chill for about 3 hours or until set.

Decorate with coffee beans or (DF) chocolate-coated coffee beans and dust with sifted cocoa powder.

Rosewater Angel Cake with Berries

This happens to be a low-fat cake, so it is ideal for weight watching dinner guests. You can use any mixture of fruit you like to suit whatever is in season.

Serves 8–12

CAKE
125g/4¹/₂oz/generous ³/₄ cup of rice flour, sifted
185g/6¹/₂oz/scant 1 cup of caster (superfine) sugar
A pinch of salt
7 large free-range egg whites
2 teaspoons of cream of tartar
1 tablespoon of rosewater

FILLING AND SAUCE
Plenty of fresh soft fruits such as strawberries,
   blackberries, blueberries, raspberries, stoned
(pitted) cherries or currants
White rum
Caster (superfine) sugar to taste

(I have left the quantities optional so that you can use
   this recipe for a small party of 6 guests or increase
   the amount of filling and sauce for the maximum of
   12 guests).

A large, deep, non-stick ring baking tin or a large,
   deep, non-stick Kugelhopf tin

Preheat the oven to 180°C/350°F/Gas mark 4

Make the cake first. Sift together the flour, 7 tablespoons of the sugar and the salt in a bowl and set aside. In another larger bowl, whisk the egg whites at low speed for 1 minute, or until they are thick and foamy. Add the cream of tartar and increase the speed to medium.

Slowly sprinkle 2 more tablespoons of sugar into the egg whites and beat them until they form soft peaks. Add the rosewater and fold in the remaining sugar, followed by the sifted flour mixture.

Pour the cake mixture into the tin and bake in the oven for about 40 minutes, or until an inserted skewer comes out clean. It should be golden and firm to touch.

Leave the cake to cool in the tin for 20 minutes, after which time the cake should come have away from the sides of the tin. Ease the cake out and turn it on to a large serving plate.

Fill the centre of the cake with as many berries as you like, so that it looks pretty. Keep the rest to make the sauce. Put plenty of berries, some rum and a little sugar into the food processor and pulse into a purée. Adjust the sweetness and the consistency to suit your taste with extra sugar, water and rum. Sieve the sauce and discard all the pips and skins.

The sauce should be just runny enough to spoon over the cake and trickle a little bit down the sides of the cake but not too runny otherwise it will trickle away!

Spoon the sauce decoratively over the sponge ring only, not on the fruit filling.

Serve the rest of the sauce in a pretty jug to accompany the pudding.

Banana and Coffee Roulade

Roulades are one of those fun things that look great but are so simple to make. As this one is not filled with cream it will keep in the refrigerator for 24 hours but it must be sealed completely in clingfilm (plastic wrap) otherwise the bananas will go brown.

Serves 8

ROULADE

100g/3¹/₂oz/²/₃ cup of rice flour
¹/₂ teaspoon of (GF) baking powder
¹/₂ teaspoon of bicarbonate of soda (baking soda)
A pinch of salt
1 large ripe banana, mashed
2 tablespoons of coconut cream
¹/₂ teaspoon of vanilla extract
1 tablespoon of white rum
85g/3oz/6 tablespoons of (DF) margarine
100g/3¹/₂oz/¹/₂ cup of caster (superfine) sugar
1 large free-range egg, lightly beaten

FILLING AND DECORATION

30g/1oz/¹/₄ cup of chopped and toasted hazelnuts,

for decoration

1 tablespoon of good instant coffee dissolved in 1 tablespoon of boiling water
1 tablespoon of white rum
100g/3¹/₂oz/7 tablespoons of (DF) margarine
200g/7oz/1¹/₂ cups of icing (confectioners') sugar
1–2 ripe small bananas, finely sliced and tossed in another tablespoon of rum (or ¹/₂ a tablespoon of lemon juice if you prefer)
Icing (confectioners') sugar, sifted for decoration

A roulade or Swiss roll tin, lined with baking parchment (wax paper)

Preheat the oven to 180°C/350°F/Gas mark 4

Make the roulade. Sift together the flour, baking powder, bicarbonate of soda (baking soda) and salt. In another bowl, mix together the banana, coconut cream, vanilla and rum.
Beat the margarine and sugar in a food processor until pale and fluffy. Slowly add the egg and then beat for about 30 seconds. Scrape the mixture into the mashed banana, mix briefly and then fold in the flour mixture.
Lightly spread the mixture in the roulade tin and bake in the oven for 15–20 minutes, or until firm to touch and golden.
Leave the roulade to cool for a couple of minutes and then turn it on to a sheet of baking parchment (wax paper) sprinkled all over with the chopped toasted hazelnuts.
Quickly peel off the baking parchment (wax paper) used during cooking and trim the edges of the roulade with a sharp knife (this stops the edges going hard, making it easier to roll up).
Cover with a clean but damp (with cold water) tea towel and set aside until cold.

Make the filling in the food processor by beating the dissolved coffee and rum with the margarine and icing (confectioners') sugar until it is smooth and light.

Have the bananas ready and then spread the coffee filling all over the roulade and cover it with the sliced bananas.

Quickly roll the roulade into a log shape and slide on to a long serving dish. Sprinkle over any nuts that have been left behind and then sift over the icing (confectioners') sugar. Serve or chill until needed.

Marbled Peach Cheesecake

This cheesecake is also delicious made with apricots or nectarines. You can replace the goat's/sheep's yogurt with soya yogurt if necessary, but it is not quite so good.

Serves 8

PEACH PURÉE
255g/9oz/1 1/2 cups ready-to-eat dried peaches
Zest of I lemon and the juice of half the lemon
55g/2oz/scant 1/4 cup of caster (superfine) sugar
Juice of 2 oranges
4 tablespoons of Cointreau

THE BASE
55g/2oz/1/2 cup of chopped toasted hazelnuts
100g/3 1/2oz of ready-made (GF) plain, flavoured
   (ie. ginger) or chocolate cookies
55g/2oz/scant 1/4 cup of caster (superfine) sugar
55g/2oz/1/4 cup of (DF) margarine, melted

THE FILLING
3 x 227g/8oz tubs of set sheep's Greek-style yogurt
   or goat's yogurt
200g/7oz/1 cup of caster (superfine) sugar
2 large free-range eggs plus 2 large free-range egg
   yolks
40g/1 1/2oz/5 tablespoons of rice flour
140ml/5fl oz/2/3 cup of coconut cream
2 fresh and ripe peaches, peeled, stoned (pitted)
   and sliced or
425g/15oz canned peach halves in natural juice,
   drained and sliced

A 23cm/9 inch-deep, fluted, ovenproof, china quiche
   dish or springform cake tin

Preheat the oven to 170°C/325°F/Gas mark 3

Place the peaches, lemon zest, sugar and 300ml/10fl oz/1 1/4 cups of water in a pan and bring slowly to the boil. Simmer for about 20 minutes so that the liquid reduces.

When the fruit is soft and mushy, allow it to cool, then liquidize with half the orange juice and half the Cointreau, so that it is very thick.

Make the base by grinding the hazelnuts, cookies and sugar in a food processor until they resemble fine breadcrumbs. Add the melted margarine and process briefly. Press the mixture down into the base of the dish. Cook the base in the oven for 5 minutes.

Beat the yogurt, sugar, eggs, flour and coconut cream together in a bowl and when it is smooth, stir in half of the peach purée to create a marbled effect throughout.

Spoon the mixture over the cooked base and level it off. Arrange the fresh or canned peaches in slices over the top – fan shapes look great.

Bake in the oven for around 50 minutes, or until the cheesecake is firm and dark golden brown. It is a good idea to turn the cheesecake around half way through baking, so that it cooks evenly.

Cool completely before refrigerating. Cover and chill until needed.

Add the remaining orange juice and Cointreau to the peach purée. Stir in enough water to make the purée suitable for pouring from a serving jug. Chill the peach purée until needed.

Serve the cheesecake from the dish with the accompanying peach purée.

Cranberry and Wine Jelly with Grapes

Mix red and white grapes for a pretty effect in this dish, or choose any fruit in season, which can be fresh or poached and then served around the jellies.

Serves 4–6

300ml/10fl oz/1¼ cups of red wine

140g/5oz/¾ cup of caster (superfine) sugar

Zest of 1 orange

1 teaspoon of mixed spice (pie spice)

1 sprig of rosemary

600ml/20fl oz/2½ cups of cranberry juice

1½ sachets (17g/¾oz/US 1½ tablespoons) of powdered gelatine

A fresh bunch of seedless grapes, trimmed, skinned and halved

2–3 tablespoons of redcurrant jelly

A little red wine or port

Juice of 1 large orange

4–6 standard ramekin dishes or tin jelly moulds, lightly brushed with oil

Stir the wine, sugar, orange zest, mixed spice (pie spice) and rosemary together in a saucepan over medium heat to gently dissolve the sugar. Bring the mixture up to the boil and boil for 5 minutes. Remove the pan from the heat, add the cranberry juice and allow the mixture to infuse for 5 minutes.

Place the saucepan back on to medium heat and bring the cranberry and wine mixture to the boil. Boil for 5 minutes, then remove from the heat and quickly stir in the gelatine. Stir from time to time until the gelatine has dissolved.

Sieve the jelly into a good pouring jug and then pour the wine jelly into the prepared ramekins. Leave the jellies to set for at least 4 hours or until firm enough to turn out.

Meanwhile, prepare as many of the grapes as you think you will need for 4 or 6 guests and put them in a bowl.

Dissolve the redcurrant jelly with the orange juice and a little extra wine or port and bring it to the boil. Adjust the consistency with more liquid or jelly if necessary – it should be just runny enough to coat the grapes. Quickly remove it from the heat and blend thoroughly until smooth. Pour it over the grapes, cool, then cover and leave it at room temperature until ready to serve. Turn out the jellies on to plates and spoon the grapes with a little of the liquid around each jelly. Serve straight away.

Chocolate and Pistachio Bavarois with Orange Sherry Sauce

This is extremely rich, so you can use smaller tin moulds and serve 8 to 10 guests instead. There is plenty of sauce to allow for this!

Serves 6

BAVAROIS
255g/9oz/1½ cups of (DF) dark continental chocolate
140g/5oz/½ cup plus 2 tablespoons of (DF)
   margarine
4 large free-range eggs
55g/2oz/scant ¼ cup of caster (superfine) sugar
100g/3½oz/¾ cup of peeled pistachio nuts
A pinch of salt

6 standard ramekins brushed with sunflower oil and
   lined with a circle of baking parchment (wax paper)

ORANGE SHERRY SAUCE
4 free-range eggs, beaten
200g/7oz/1 cup of caster (superfine) sugar
Grated zest of 1 orange
140ml/5fl oz/⅔ cup of fresh orange juice
55g/2oz/¼ cup of (DF) margarine, cut into small
   pieces
60ml/2fl oz/¼ cup of pale dry sherry or Marsala

1–2 oranges, pith and pips removed and cut into
   segments for decoration or poached, sliced
   kumquats or fresh physalis fruit (Cape
   gooseberries), and (DF) cream, to decorate

Melt the chocolate with the margarine in a large bowl in the microwave until just soft. Stir the mixture until smooth.

Separate the eggs and put the whites in a very large bowl. Place the yolks and the sugar in a food processor and beat until thick and creamy. Stir this into the chocolate mixture, followed by the nuts.

Beat the egg whites and salt together until soft peaks form. Fold the egg whites into the chocolate mixture using a metal spoon, then divide the mixture between the prepared ramekins.

Cover with clingfilm (plastic wrap) and chill for at least 4 hours, or until firmly set.

Meanwhile, make the sauce. Put all the ingredients, except the margarine and sherry, into a food processor and beat for a few seconds.

Transfer the mixture into a non-stick saucepan and cook over low heat until the mixture thickens to a custard. Keep stirring so that it does not stick to the pan – do not boil the custard or it will separate. Quickly beat in the margarine and sherry. Transfer to a bowl and allow to cool, then cover and chill until needed.

To serve, peel the clingfilm (plastic wrap) off the pudddings, dip the ramekins briefly in hot water to loosen the bavarois, then turn them out on to the centre of each plate, pour the orange and sherry sauce around each one and decorate with a couple of orange segments, poached kumquats or fresh physalis fruit (Cape gooseberries) with their wings peeled back. Swirl little drops of (DF) cream into the sauce if desired.

Cherry Chocolate Torte

Another blissful combination – cherries, brandy and chocolate! Here it is taken from the past, a Black Forest Gâteau to a trendy modern style of cooking, a torte. Serve with lashings of crème fraîche (not DF) or (DF) vanilla ice-cream.

Serves 6–8

BASE
155g/5¹/₂oz/1¹/₃ cups of (GF) ratafias (almond macaroon cookies)
2 tablespoons of (DF) cocoa powder
55g/2oz/¹/₄ cup of (DF) margarine, melted

CAKE
The same weight of 2 large free-range eggs (in their shells), caster (superfine) sugar
(DF) margarine and rice flour
3 tablespoons of (DF) cocoa powder
3 tablespoons of cherry/brandy liqueur or of good quality brandy
1 teaspoon of (GF) baking powder
100g/3¹/₂oz/1¹/₄ cups of glacé cherries halved and soaked in brandy for 24 hours if possible, or a small jar of cherries in brandy, drained but brandy retained
85/g/3oz/³/₄ cup of pine nuts
Extra caster (superfine) sugar for sprinkling

A 23cm/9 inch round loose-bottomed, spring-release cake tin, lined with baking parchment (wax paper)

Preheat the oven to 180°C/350°F/Gas mark 4

Process the ratafias in the food processor until they resemble breadcrumbs. Add the cocoa and melted margarine and mix well. Transfer to the prepared dish and press down firmly to form an even base. Bake in the oven for 5 minutes.

First weigh the eggs, then weigh exactly the same weight of sugar, followed by the margarine and then the flour. Beat the sugar and margarine together until light and fluffy in a food processor. Beat in the cocoa powder and then the eggs, one at a time. Add the cherry/brandy liqueur or brandy, briefly blend in the flour and quickly stir in the baking powder.

Gently stir in the cherries, then spoon the mixture into the prepared cake tin. Carefully level off the cake, scatter the pine nuts over it and sprinkle with a little extra sugar.

Bake the cake in the oven for 35 minutes, or until the nuts are golden and the cake is firm to touch.

Allow the cake cool down in the tin before easing it out and removing the baking parchment (wax paper). Place the cake on a plate and serve warm or cold.

Lemon Curd Ice-cream

This is such a refreshing ice-cream that I often make large quantities. It is perfect for bigger parties outside in the garden in the summer or barbecues for teenagers.

Serves about 16

LEMON CURD
Zest and juice from 4 unwaxed lemons
4 large free-range eggs and 4 large free-range egg yolks
300g/10½oz/1½ cups of caster (superfine) sugar
200g/7oz/1 cup of (DF) margarine

ICE-CREAM
100g/3½oz/1 cup of chopped citrus peel soaked in 2 tablespoons of Cointreau for up to 24 hours before use
4 or 5 x 227g/8oz tubs of thick sheep's yogurt
All the lemon curd
2 large free-range egg whites

Make the lemon curd first (this can be made up to a week in advance and kept sealed in the refrigerator). Beat the lemon zest and juice with the eggs, egg yolks and sugar in a non-stick saucepan. Place on medium heat and stir the mixture until it warms up and the sugar dissolves. Bring the mixture to boiling point but do not boil, it should be very thick. Remove from the heat immediately, tip in all the margarine and stir vigorously until it is thoroughly incorporated. Stir frequently while the lemon curd cools down. Transfer to a sealable container and chill until needed. The curd must be cold before it is added to the ice-cream.

Marinate the citrus peel in a little bowl, the day before if possible. Kep it cool and covered until needed.

Make sure your ice-cream maker is ready when you want to make the ice-cream. If you like a strong lemon flavour then use the smaller amount of yogurt and if you prefer it a little less zingy then use the 5 tubs.

Whisk the yogurt with the lemon curd in a very large mixing bowl for at least 6 minutes at medium speed. It will become lighter and slightly increased in volume.

Whisk the egg whites until very stiff and then fold into the curd mixture. Fold in the citrus peel and Cointreau.

Churn the ice-cream in 2 batches until frozen. Transfer to a sealable container and freeze until needed.

You can either buy little (GF) meringue nests to serve the ice-cream in for dinner parties or you can make (GF) brandy snap baskets, which are in my cookbook *The Sensitive Gourmet* for a special effect.

CHAPTER 4

Cookies, Cakes and Sweets

Melt-in-the-mouth cookies are perfect to serve with ice-creams. Fresh, crumbly and warm, cookies are a family favourite – destined to vanish like lightning well before they ever reach a cookie jar!

My grandmother's cakes were always as light as air. As children we used to queue up in the kitchen to lick the pudding bowl clean of her wondrous mixtures. We used to plead for sticky chocolate cakes and gooey banana cake and would make a thorough nuisance of ourselves until we were allowed to don our aprons and do magnificent things with our wooden spoons! So in memory of her, I have selected some of our favourite recipes and some new ones which I know will be just as popular.

There is a rich spicy fruitcake that can be transformed into a wedding, christening, Christmas or anniversary cake with a flourish of icing and little cakes and cookies which are ideal for children's tea parties, so that there will be something for everyone.

Fruit or vegetable purées can be an excellent way of cutting down on using fat and sugar and at the same time they manage to accentuate the flavours. Anyone who doubts that feather light cakes can be made without gluten is going to be thrilled and surprised when they taste the recipes in this book.

My culinary skills have never extended to making sweets to nibble with coffee. Mainly I suspect because I just go and buy a bar of wicked dark chocolate for my chocoholic fix! But here are a few recipes that can be adapted to seasonal fresh or crystallized fruit for special occasions. Sometimes I do make them on their own merit as an unusual pudding. Everybody loves them, feeling perhaps that this indulgence is marginally less naughty than a full-blown pudding being devoured. However, if this is not an appealing thought there are tempting chocolates available by mail order and an address is listed on page 136.

Finally, these sweets make imaginative gifts for family and friends. Carefully placed in little paper cups, these sweets can be arranged in charming boxes and tied up with pretty ribbons to amuse and delight all ages.

Peanut Butter Cookies

You can add chunks of (DF) dark chocolate to vary these cookies. I find them remarkably efficient as bribery when my God-children come to stay!

Makes 24

100g/3¹/₂oz/²/₃ cup of rice flour
130g/4¹/₂oz/generous ³/₄ cup of maize flour
¹/₂ teaspoon of salt
¹/₂ teaspoon of bicarbonate of soda (baking soda)
100g/3¹/₂oz/7 tablespoons of (DF) margarine
130g/4¹/₂oz/¹/₂ cup of (GF/DF) crunchy peanut butter

170g/6oz/³/₄ cup of soft brown sugar
2 large free-range eggs
1 teaspoon of Madagascan vanilla extract
1 teaspoon of water
100g/3¹/₂oz/¹/₂ cup of dry-roasted peanuts

Preheat oven to 180°C/350°F/Gas mark 4

Sift the flours with the salt and baking soda on to a plate and set aside. In a large bowl, cream the margarine, peanut butter and sugar until soft and light. Gently mix in half the eggs, the vanilla and water, and then stir in half the flour. Repeat so that they are all used up, then add the peanuts. Drop heaped spoonfuls of the dough on to non-stick baking trays and press with the back of a floured fork to flatten slightly.
Bake them for 15 minutes. Allow the cookies to cool a little on the tray, before transferring them to a wire rack to cool completely.

Banana and Chocolate Chip Cookies

This is such a good way of using up brown, over ripe bananas that no one else in the house will eat.

Makes 24

170g/6oz/1¼ cups of rice flour
170g/6oz/1¼ cups of oat flour (or finely processed oats)
1 heaped teaspoon of bicarbonate of soda (baking soda)
A pinch of salt
255g/9oz/1 cup plus 2 tablespoons of (DF) margarine, diced

140g/5oz/¾ cup of demerara sugar
100g/3½oz/½ cup of granulated sugar
2 large free-range eggs
1 teaspoon of Madagascan vanilla extract
2 small ripe bananas, mashed
85g/3oz/¾ cup of banana chips, roughly broken up
115g/4oz/⅔ cup of (DF) dark chocolate drops or chopped pieces

Preheat the oven to 190°C/375°F/Gas mark 5

Sift the flours, bicarbonate of soda (baking soda) and salt into a bowl and set aside. In a food processor, beat the margarine and both the sugars until light and fluffy. Gradually add the eggs, followed by the vanilla. Transfer the mixture to a large bowl, stir in the mashed bananas and fold in the flour as lightly as you can. Fold in the banana chips and chocolate pieces.
Drop tablespoons of the mixture on to a non-stick baking tray, spacing the cookies well apart. Bake them for 15 minutes, or until golden brown.
Cool the cookies slightly before lifting them on to a wire rack. When they are cold, store in an airtight container until needed.

Coffee and Brazil Nut Squares

These cookies are a slight variation of traditional brownies. They freeze well, which is always handy in the school holidays.

Makes 12

85g/3oz/6 tablespoons of (DF) margarine
200g/7oz/1 cup of demerara sugar
1130g/4½oz/generous ¾ cup of rice flour
1½ teaspoons of (GF) baking powder
Pinch of salt
2 large free-range eggs, lightly beaten
1 teaspoon of Madagascan vanilla extract
1 heaped teaspoon of instant coffee, dissolved in 1 tablespoon of boiling water

1 tablespoon of (DF) cocoa powder, dissolved in 1 tablespoon of boiling water
55g/2oz/½ cup of Brazil nuts, roughly chopped and lightly dusted with rice flour
85g/3oz/½ cup of (DF &GF) dark chocolate drops or pieces

18 x 25.5cm/10 inch and 3cm/1¼-inch deep baking tin lightly oiled

Preheat the oven to 190°C/375°F/Gas mark 5

Heat the margarine and sugar together in a pan until it begins to dissolve, then remove from the heat and allow to cool.

Sift the flour, baking powder and salt into a bowl. Mix together the eggs, vanilla, coffee and dissolved cocoa in another bowl. Stir the egg mixture into the margarine mixture and then fold in the flour mixture.

Lightly stir in the nuts and chocolate drops or pieces, then pour the mixture into the prepared tin. Bake for 20 minutes, or until the sides are coming away from the edges of the tin. Leave the cake to cool in the tin. When cold, carefully cut the cake into 12 squares and serve, or store in an airtight container until needed.

Coconut and Cinnamon Flapjacks

Perfect flapjacks should be hard enough to keep their shape without crumbling but gooey enough to have a chewy texture. I alternate taking these to work for lunch with the Coffee and Brazil Nut Squares on page 94.

Makes 12

200g/7oz/1 cup less 2 tablespoons of (DF) margarine

300g/11oz/scant 1 cup of golden syrup (corn syrup)

395g/14oz/4 cups of porridge oats

85g/3oz/1 cup of desiccated (shredded) coconut

85g/3oz/²/₃ cup of plump sultanas (golden raisins)

1 heaped teaspoon of ground cinnamon

Grease and line with baking parchment (wax paper) a non-stick 23cm/9-inch x 33cm/13 inch Swiss roll or roulade tin

---

Preheat the oven to 190°C/375°F/Gas mark 5

Melt the margarine with the syrup in a saucepan over medium heat. Add the oats, coconut, sultanas (golden raisins) and cinnamon. Stir the mixture until melted and well blended, then pour it into the roulade tin.

Press the mixture down into the tin, then bake for about 25 minutes, or until golden brown.

Cut the flapjacks into squares whilst still warm, but leave them to cool in the tin.

Store the flapjacks in an airtight container until needed.

Almond Petit Fours

Here are perfect little petit fours to nibble with coffee or to accompany ice-cream or sorbet as a pudding. They are also good finely crushed and mixed into meringue or vanilla ice-cream. You can freeze them or keep them for up to a week in a sealable container.

Serves about 20

220g/7oz/1 ½ cups of whole skinned almonds
255g/9oz/1 ¼ cups of caster (superfine) sugar
½ a finely grated orange
2 medium free-range egg whites

20 large glacé cherries, halved

Icing (confectioners') sugar to dust
Sheets of rice paper

Preheat the oven to 180°C/350°F/Gas mark 4

Put the almonds in a food processor and grind briefly. Add half the caster (superfine) sugar and grind again until it becomes a powder. Mix with the remaining caster (superfine) sugar and the grated orange zest. Transfer the mixture to a bowl.

In another bowl, whisk the egg whites lightly with an electric whisk, then stir the egg whites into the almond mixture to bind it.

Take heaped teaspoons of the mixture and roll it into balls, on a board dusted with icing (confectioners') sugar.

Flatten the balls with a palette knife and press half a cherry into the centre of each.

Place them well apart on a baking sheet lined with rice paper.

Bake for 15 minutes or until just firm but pale golden brown.

Cool on the baking sheets and then trim the rice paper around the biscuits. Serve the petit fours on the day of baking, dusted with icing (confectioners') sugar.

Chocolate Macaroons

These are the perfect accompaniment to lots of different types of ice-cream. The macaroons are quick to make so they are also an ideal foundation for trifles and mousse-cakes.

Makes 24

200g/7oz/1 ¹/₃ cups of whole almonds
55g/2oz/1 ¹/₃ cups of (DF) plain chocolate
130g/4¹/₂oz/¹/₂ cups plus 2 tablespoons of caster
   (superfine) sugar
1 teaspoon of Madagascan vanilla extract
¹/₂ teaspoon of almond essence

1 tablespoon of (DF) cocoa powder
2 large free-range egg whites

Icing (confectioners') sugar for dusting your hands and
   the board
Sheets of rice paper

Preheat the oven to 180°C/350°F/Gas mark 4

Bake the almonds for a few minutes until pale gold. Allow them to cool. Gently melt the chocolate in a bowl in the microwave.

Grind the cooled nuts in a food processor to a fine powder. Add the caster (superfine) sugar, vanilla extract, almond essence, cocoa powder, melted chocolate and egg whites and mix to a soft paste.

Put plenty of icing (confectioners') sugar on a clean board and roll the mixture into a long sausage. With plenty of icing (confectioners') sugar on your hands, shape slices of the dough into balls the size of walnuts.

Arrange the macaroons on sheets of rice paper on some non-stick baking trays and bake for 15 minutes, or until just firm.

Cool the cookies slightly and then cut the rice paper around the cookies and cool them on a wire rack. These macaroons are best eaten on the day of baking.

Gingerbread Men

These traditional cookies can be made into wonderful ornamental decorations at Christmas. Children love to pipe icing on to the gingerbread men.

Makes 20

100ml/3^1/$_2$ fl oz/^{1}/$_3$ cup of black treacle (molasses)

55g/2oz/^{1}/$_4$ cup of (DF) margarine

55g/2oz/scant ^{1}/$_4$ cup of unrefined dark Mauritian sugar

1 teaspoon of bicarbonate of soda (baking soda)

^{1}/$_2$ teaspoon of ground allspice

^{1}/$_2$ teaspoon of ground cinnamon

^{1}/$_2$ teaspoon of ground cloves

1 teaspoon of ground ginger

1 large free-range egg

130g/4^1/$_2$oz/generous ^{3}/$_4$ cup of rice flour

100g/3^1/$_2$oz/^{2}/$_3$ cup of millet flour

100g/3^1/$_2$oz/^{2}/$_3$ cup of potato flour

Icing if used – (GF) ready to pipe varieties, silver balls or other (GF/DF) decorations

Preheat the oven to 180°C/350°F/Gas mark 4

In a large bowl, combine the treacle (molasses) and margarine, then melt them together in the microwave. Allow the mixture to cool down, then add the sugar, bicarbonate of soda (baking soda), spices, egg and all the flours.

Beat with a wooden spoon for 2 minutes. Transfer the dough on to a floured board and knead the dough with a little extra flour until you can roll it with a floured rolling pin. Roll out the dough until it is thin enough to cut out the shapes you require. You can use any shape cutters – gingerbread men, Father Christmas, Christmas trees, hearts or stars.

Place the gingerbread men on non-stick baking trays at least 1cm/^{1}/$_2$ inch apart. Bake for 12 minutes, or until the edges are firm.

Cool on the trays before lifting them off. Transfer the gingerbread men to wire racks to cool completely.

Pipe decorative outlines with the icing and decorate with silver balls or anything you fancy, as long as you check that the ingredients are compatible with you. The icing will take about 1 hour to dry.

The gingerbread men will keep for a couple of days if stored in an airtight container.

Chocolate Shortbread Fingers

If you can eat dairy products then you can use milk chocolate, which most children prefer.

Makes 6–12

SHORTBREAD

225g/8oz/1 generous cup of caster (superfine) sugar
225g/8oz/2½ cups of ground almonds
225g/8oz/1½ cups of instant quick-cook polenta
  (maize)
225g/8oz/1 cup of (DF) margarine
1 teaspoon of almond essence

CHOCOLATE TOPPING

140g/5oz/scant cup of (DF) dark chocolate, broken
  into pieces
4 tablespoons of weak black coffee
1 teaspoon of sunflower oil
100g/3½oz/¾ cup of sifted icing (confectioners') sugar

A roulade or Swiss roll non-stick baking tin, lined with
  baking parchment (wax paper)

Preheat the oven to 170°C/325°F/Gas mark 3

Mix all the shortbread ingredients together in a bowl or a food processor until well blended.
Press the mixture evenly into the tin and bake it for 25 minutes until golden and firm to touch.
Cool the shortbread in the tin, then turn it out on to a clean surface and remove the paper.
Melt the chocolate with the coffee in the microwave and stir in the sunflower oil. Beat in the icing (confectioners') sugar and once it is glossy, spread the chocolate over the shortbread.
Make any patterns and squiggles you like to decorate it. Cut the shortbread into fingers or squares and leave it to set in a cool place.
Transfer the shortbread to an airtight container until needed.

Orange Maple Cookies

These richly flavoured Canadian-style cookies use maple syrup, but for a cheaper version substitute honey.

Serves 12

100g/3¹/₂oz/²/₃ cup of rice flour
100g/3¹/₂oz/²/₃ cup of maize flour
100g/3¹/₂oz/²/₃ cup of millet flour
115g/4oz/¹/₃ cup (DF) margarine, softened
70g/2¹/₂oz/¹/₃ cup of unrefined dark Mauritian sugar
4 tablespoons of pure maple syrup
1 teaspoon of (GF) cream of tartar

¹/₂ teaspoon of (GF) bicarbonate of soda (baking soda)
1 large free-range egg
1 tablespoon of grated orange rind

Grease and flour 2 non-stick baking trays.

Preheat the oven to 180°C/350°F/Gas mark 4

In a large bowl, mix all the ingredients with an electric whisk. When the mixture has formed a dough, shape into a ball with your hands and then wrap in clingfilm (plastic wrap) and refrigerate for 1 hour.

Roll out the dough, half at a time, until about 3mm/¹/₈-inch thick. Cut into the required shapes and place 2.5cm/1 inch apart on the trays. Bake the cookies for 10 minutes, or until they are golden.

Transfer on to wire racks to cool. Store the cookies in an airtight container until needed.

Valentine Hearts

These eye-catching little hearts make a fun gift, or amusing cookies to serve with ice-cream or mousses on St. Valentine's day.

Makes 2¹/₂–3¹/₂ dozen

100g/3¹/₂oz/¹/₂ cup of (DF) dark chocolate	140g/5oz/³/₄ cup of caster (superfine) sugar
170g/6oz/1¹/₄ cups of rice flour	
170g/6oz/1¹/₄ cups of millet flour	2 non-stick baking sheets
170g/6oz/³/₄ cup of (DF) margarine	2 heart-shaped cutters, one 5cm/2 inch and the other
1 tablespoon of strong black coffee	2.5cm/1 inch
2 teaspoons of (GF) baking powder	(fluted circular cutters can be used instead)
1 large free-range egg	

Preheat the oven to 180°C/350°F/Gas mark 4

Gently melt the chocolate in a bowl in the microwave and then stir it until smooth.

In a food processor, combine the flours and margarine with the coffee for a few seconds. Add the baking powder, egg and sugar, and process again briefly.

Shape the dough into a ball, divide into two and wrap one in clingfilm (plastic wrap). Chill the wrapped dough for 25 minutes in the freezer.

Mix the melted chocolate into the remaining dough and bring it back into a ball shape by kneading gently on a floured surface. Wrap the chocolate dough in clingfilm (plastic wrap) and freeze for 15 minutes.

Unwrap both balls of dough and divide each in half to make it easier to roll out.

Now roll out a chocolate dough and a plain dough on separate, floured boards until they are thin enough to cut out without breaking up.

Using the large heart cutter first, cut out plenty of hearts in the chocolate pastry, then using the smaller heart cutter, cut out the centre of the chocolate hearts and put them to one side.

Repeat this with the plain dough. Now gently place the smaller hearts inside the larger ones, alternating doughs so that you have a chocolate exterior and a plain interior and a plain exterior and a chocolate interior.

Bake the hearts on the trays for about 10 minutes, or until golden. Allow them to cool for a couple of minutes before transferring to wire wracks.

Chocolate Marshmallow Crispies

Children on school holidays with time on their hands and a sense of creativity can try making these simple cookies for tea.

Makes 12

170g/6oz/³/₄ cup of (DF) margarine

140g/5oz/scant cup of (DF) chocolate

85g/3oz/¹/₄ cup of golden syrup (corn syrup)

140g/5oz/4¹/₂ cups of (WF) rice crispies (puffed rice cereal)

170g/6oz/1¹/₂cups of rolled oats

100g/3¹/₂oz/2 cups of chopped up or mini marshmallows

Place the margarine, chocolate and syrup in a non-stick saucepan and heat gently until melted and blended together.

Cool the mixture before adding the rice crispies, oats and marshmallows.

Mix well and then press the crispies into 12 paper baking cups or a 20cm/8 inch square non-stick baking tin.

Chill for 30 minutes and mark out portions in the tin. Chill for at least 2 hours in the freezer before serving. Keep the crispies cool otherwise there will be lots of very sticky fingers!

Nutmeg Cookies

You can use any spice you like for these little cookies – simply change it according to the type of fruits,
mousses or ices you are serving.

Makes 30

200g/7oz/1 cup less 2 tablespoons of (DF) margarine
85g/3oz/generous ¹/₂ cup of icing (confectioners')
  sugar
100g/3¹/₂oz/²/₃ cup of rice flour
100g/3¹/₂oz/²/₃ cup of (GF) cornflour (cornstarch)
55g/2oz/²/₃ cup of ground almonds

1 teaspoon of finely grated nutmeg
Finely grated zest of ¹/₂ a lemon

Line a couple of baking trays with baking parchment
  (wax paper)
Extra flour for dusting hands and board

Preheat the oven to 180°C/350°F/Gas mark 4

Cream the margarine and icing (confectioners') sugar in a food processor, then add all the
remaining ingredients, giving them a quick blend until a dough forms.
With floured hands, wrap the ball of dough in clingfilm (plastic wrap) and chill for 2 hours.
Roll the dough into a long sausage shape on a floured board and cut it into 30 slices. Place the
slices on the prepared tray, making sure that the cookies have room to expand.
Bake the cookies for about 15 minutes, or until lightly coloured around the edges.
Cool the cookies slightly, then transfer them to wire tray to cool.
Store the cookies in an airtight container until needed.

Rainbow Tarts

This is a special request from a little boy in Scotland who finds children's tea parties a sad affair because he can not eat wheat or nuts, so there are several recipes in this section just for him.

Makes 18

PASTRY	FILLING
200g/7oz/scant 1½ cups of the Stamp Collection (WF) flour	About a teaspoon of different coloured jam (jelly), for best effect, for example, raspberry, apricot, gooseberry, blackberry
55g/2oz/½ cup of sifted icing (confectioners') sugar	
A pinch of salt	
100g/3½oz/7 tablespoons of (DF) margarine	3 x 6 non-stick bun trays, each lined with a circle of baking parchment (wax paper)
1 large free-range egg	

Preheat the oven to 180°C/350°F/Gas mark 4

Make the pastry by mixing all the ingredients together in a food processor briefly but just enough to gather the dough into a ball.

Roll out the pastry on a floured board, cut into large enough circles to fit your tart tins and press a pastry circle into each tin.

Choose a variety of jam (jelly) and place a spoonful of the selected jam (jelly) into the centre of each tart.

Bake the jam (jelly) tarts for 20 minutes or until the pastry is golden.

Cool the tarts in the tins and then ease them out and on to a wire rack.

Store in an airtight container until needed.

Little Apple Tarts

I always keep a jar of apple purée in the cupboard because it is marvellous for instant tarts, mousses and sauces.

Makes 18

PASTRY
200g/7oz/scant 1 1/2 cups of the Stamp Collection (WF) flour
55g/2oz/1/2 cup of sifted icing (confectioners') sugar
A pinch of salt
100g/3 1/2oz/7 tablespoons of (DF) margarine
1 large free-range egg

FILLING
12 heaped tablespoons of organic ready-made apple purée (sweetened with honey)

3 large free-range egg yolks
Freshly grated nutmeg
1/2 teaspoon of ground cinnamon
1/2 teaspoon of mixed spice (pie spice)
1 small dessert apple, peeled, quartered, cored and sliced very thinly
A little lemon juice

3 x 6 non-stick bun trays, each lined with a circle of baking parchment (wax paper)

Preheat the oven to 180°C/350°F/Gas mark 4

Make the pastry by mixing all the ingredients together in a food processor briefly but just enough to gather the dough into a ball.
Roll out the pastry on a floured board and cut into large enough circles to fit your tart tins. Press each pastry circle into the prepared tins.
Mix the apple purée and egg yolks in a bowl with a little grated nutmeg, cinnamon and mixed spice (pie spice). Prepare the apple and brush each slice with a tiny amount of lemon juice.
Place about three quarters of a tablespoonful of the apple purée into the centre of each tart.
Decorate with one slice of the apple, pressed slightly into the purée.
Bake the tarts for 30 minutes, or until the apple is just browned at the edges, the filling is set and the pastry golden.
Cool in the tins and then ease them out and on to wire racks. Eat on the day of baking or keep in the refrigerator so that they do not go soggy.

Chocolate and Cinnamon Birthday Cake

Try using novelty chocolates to decorate this enticing birthday cake. A very good selection of dairy-free and gluten-free chocolates is from the mail order company listed on page 136.

Serves 10–20

CAKE
550g/1lb 3oz/3¼ cups of (DF) plain chocolate, broken into pieces
310g/11oz/1⅓ cups of (DF) margarine
2 teaspoons of ground cinnamon
570ml/20fl oz/2½ cups of boiling water
395g/14oz/2 cups of caster (superfine) sugar
3 large free-range eggs, beaten
200g/7oz/scant 1½ cups of rice flour
200g/7oz/scant 1½ cups of millet flour
3 teaspoons of (GF) baking powder
1 teaspoon of bicarbonate of soda (baking soda)

CAKE ICING
300g/10½oz/2 cups of icing (confectioners') sugar, sifted

75ml/2½ fl oz/¼ cup of orange liqueur or brandy (alternatively for children use weak coffee)
100ml/3½ fl oz/⅓ cup of soya cream

PIPING ICING
A dash of boiling water to melt 2 heaped tablespoons of (DF) cocoa powder
140g/5oz/1 cup of sifted icing (confectioners') sugar
140g/5oz/½ cup plus 2 tablespoons of (DF) margarine

Candles or novelty chocolates to decorate

Grease and line with baking parchment (wax paper) a 24.5cm/9½ inch, loose-bottomed, spring release, round cake tin and a 30cm/12 inch round silver paper cake board.

Preheat the oven to 170°C/325°F/Gas mark 3

Make the cake first. Place 350g/12oz/2 cups of the chocolate in a bowl with 225g/8oz/1 cup of the margarine, the cinnamon and the boiling water, and carefully melt in the microwave. Stir until smooth, then stir in the sugar and beaten eggs.
Fold in the flours, the baking powder and bicarbonate of soda (baking soda) very briefly.
Spoon the mixture into the prepared tin and bake in the centre of the oven for 50 minutes, or until the centre of the cake is just firm. An inserted skewer should come out clean.
Leave the cake to cool down in the tin and then remove it from the tin on to a wire rack to cool completely.
Make the cake icing by heating the remaining 200g/7oz/1¼ cups of chocolate with the remaining 100g/3½oz/7 tablespoons margarine in a bowl in the microwave. Stir in the icing (confectioners') sugar, liqueur and soya cream, and beat until smooth and blended.
Place the cake on the centre of the cake board and spread it all over with the icing. Use a palette

knife for a clean finish and work quickly as the icing sets pretty fast.

Make up the piping icing. (For a smooth and light icing, ensure that the boiling water just makes the cocoa melt.) Put all the piping icing ingredients together in a food processor and beat until smooth and just soft enough to pipe around the cake.

Fill a clean piping bag fitted with a rosette or shell-style nozzle with the piping icing and carefully pipe rosettes or shells all around the base and top of the cake.

Decorate the cake when the icing has set, according to the age of the recipient – candles or chocolates!

Passion Cake

I have absolutely no idea why carrot cakes are often called passion cakes but perhaps the idea of carrots seems too worthy and off putting! Whatever the reason this passion cake is delicious.

Serves 8–10

240g/8½oz/1¾ cups of the (WF) Stamp Collection flour

480g/17oz/2½ cups cups caster (superfine) sugar

2 heaped teaspoons of (GF) baking powder

2 heaped teaspoons of ground cinnamon

240ml/8fl oz/1 cup of corn oil

3 large free-range eggs, beaten

2 teaspoons of Madagascan vanilla extract

455g/1lb/3¼ cups of carrots (peeled weight), cooked and puréed

115g/4oz/1 cup of chopped walnuts

85g/3oz/1 cup of shredded coconut

170g/6oz/¾ cup of canned crushed pineapple, drained

85g/3oz/½ cup of plump sultanas (golden raisins)

SOFT ICING AND FILLING

250g/9oz/1 cup plus 2 tablespoons of (DF) margarine

395g/14oz/3 cups of icing (confectioners') sugar

Grated zest and juice of 1 small orange

1 tablespoon of orange liqueur

1 tablespoon of orange flower water

4 tablespoons of toasted coconut pieces

Two 23cm/9 inch non-stick cake tins, lined with baking parchment (wax paper)

Preheat the oven to 180°C/350°F/Gas mark 4

Sift the flour, sugar, baking powder and cinnamon into a bowl. Add the oil, eggs and vanilla, and beat well. Fold in the carrots, walnuts, coconut, pineapple and sultanas (golden raisins).

Divide the batter evenly between the two prepared tins. Bake the cakes for about an hour or until the edges have come away from the sides of the tins and the cake is firm.

Leave the cakes to cool in the tins, then turn on to wire racks, remove the paper and let them get completely cold.

Make the icing by beating the margarine with the icing (confectioners') sugar until light and fluffy. Beat in the orange zest, orange juice and liqueur until smooth. Carefully beat in the orange flower water. The icing should be soft and light but you have to beat in all the ingredients a little at a time to avoid curdling the icing. If it begins to separate, quickly add more icing (confectioners') sugar and beat until smooth.

Place one cake on a serving plate and spread the one third of the filling over it, then cover the filling with the remaining cake. Decorate the cake with the remaining two thirds of the filling, spreading it lightly all over the cake.

Sprinkle the toasted coconut all over the cake and keep it in a cool place until ready to serve.

Lemon Curd Cake

This lovely cake is perfect for a serene English afternoon tea under an old shady tree.

Serves 6–8

LEMON CURD

4 large lemons with good skins
8 large free-range egg yolks, beaten
100g/3½oz/7 tablespoons of (DF) margarine
340g/12oz/1⅔ cups of caster (superfine) sugar

CAKE

170g/6oz/¾ cup of (DF) margarine
170g/6oz/1 cup less 2 tablespoons of caster (superfine) sugar
3 large free-range eggs
Grated zest of 1 large lemon

Juice of ½ the lemon
100g/3½oz/⅔ cup of rice flour, sifted
70g/2½oz/½ cup of maize flour, sifted
2 teaspoons of (GF) baking powder

LEMON ICING

Zest of 1 lemon
Juice of ½ a lemon
140g/5oz/1 cup of icing (confectioners') sugar, sifted

A greased and floured non-stick 23cm/9-inch deep, round cake tin

---

Preheat the oven to 180°/350°F/Gas Mark 4

First make the lemon curd. Grate the zest of the 4 lemons, then squeeze the juice and put both ingredients into a non-stick saucepan on extremely low heat. Add the lightly beaten eggs, margarine and sugar and stir until sugar has dissolved. Continue cooking until the lemon curd thickens. Pour the lemon curd into clean, hot, dry jam (jelly) jars and seal. Cool and refrigerate the lemon curd and use within 4 weeks.

To make the cake, cream the margarine and sugar in a food processor until pale and fluffy. Transfer the mixture to a large bowl and beat in the eggs, a little at a time, with the zest and juice. Gently fold in the flours and baking powder. Spoon the batter into the prepared tin, smooth the top and bake the cake for 25 minutes. Cool the cake slightly, then ease it out of the tin and peel off the baking parchment (wax paper).

When the cake is cold, slice it in half horizontally, and place the base of the cake on a serving plate. Spread the cake with plenty of lemon curd and cover with the other half of the cake. Finally, mix all the ingredients for the lemon icing to a smooth, thick paste and drizzle over the top of the cake.

Keep the cake in the refrigerator until needed, but serve at room temperature.

If you don't want to make lemon icing, dust the cake with icing (confectioners') sugar only or squeeze juice and seeds or 3–4 ripe passion fruit and then dust with icing (confectioners') sugar. Scrumptious also with blueberries, strawberries or raspberries on top and dusted with icing (confectioners') sugar.

Orange Cake with Marshmallow Topping

This recipe, given to me by some American friends, suits all ages and seasons. The exact weight of the three eggs in the recipe determines the amount of sugar, margarine and flour needed.

Serves 8–10

The same weight of;
3 large free-range eggs (in their shells), of caster (superfine) sugar, (DF) margarine and (GF) flour – rice flour and maize flour or millet flour or (WF) flour – barley flour, or any of the above flours in equal parts
Grated zest and juice of 2 large oranges
2 heaped teaspoons of (GF) baking powder
70g/2¹/₂oz/1¹/₂ cups of miniature marshmallows or

ordinary marshmallows halved
225g/8oz/1¹/₂ cups of icing (confectioners') sugar, sifted

Grease and line with baking parchment (wax paper) an 20cm/8 inch deep-sided, non-stick, round cake tin
A long skewer for securing the cake

Preheat the oven to 190°C/375°F/Gas mark 5

First make the cake. Blend the sugar and margarine in a food processor until light and fluffy. Add three quarters of the orange juice and zest, and blend briefly. Add half the flour and mix briefly. Break the whole eggs into a bowl and whisk with a fork. Now add half the egg to the mixture in the food processor and whizz briefly. Add the remaining egg and whizz again. Briefly mix in the remaining flour and the baking powder.

Spoon the mixture into the tin, bake for 15 minutes, then reduce the oven temperature to 180°C/350°F/Gas mark 4 and bake for another 15 minutes, or until well risen, golden and firm to touch.

Leave the cake to cool for 10 minutes in the tin, then turn on to a plate. Peel off the baking parchment (wax paper) and leave the cake to stand, upside down, for 10 minutes.

Carefully tip the cake, so it is topside up, on to a serving plate.

Slice the cake in half horizontally, cover with marshmallows, then immediately cover the marshmallows with the remaining layer of cake.

Secure the cake by inserting a long skewer through the centre of the cake. Set aside to allow the warm cake to melt the marshmallows.

Now make the icing by gradually mixing the remaining orange juice and zest into a bowl of the sifted icing (confectioners') sugar and beating until smooth. You may not need all the juice, so add a little at a time.

Spread the icing over the cake (having removed the skewer) and chill it until it is set.

Serve the cake at room temperature but cover and return to the refrigerator for storage – if there is any left!

Wedding Cake

This is the cake that we made for my wheat and dairy free wedding in the Spring. It had elegant white icing, so to give it some extra decoration we wrapped the cake in beautiful gold ribbon and finished it with a bouquet of perfect white roses on the top. It was very simple and effective and was admired by everyone at the reception.

Serves 100–150 guests

If you want to have traditional columns and tiers, ornate icing and decoration, I suggest that you make the cake, let it mature and cover it with the marzipan. Then take it to an expert and have it professionally iced, decorated and delivered to your reception.

EQUIPMENT

3 square cake tins: 32cm/12½ inch; 25cm/10 inch; 16.5cm/6½ inch

1 x 41cm/16-inch square silver paper cake board

2 matching smaller square silver paper cake boards with about 2.5cm/1 inch spare border around both cakes.

White, gold, silver or coloured silk ribbon of your choice

Fresh or silk flowers, or other suitable decoration for the top of the cake

Non-stick (wax) paper and tin foil to line the tins, extra (DF) margarine for greasing

Icing equipment if you need it (piping bags, nozzles etc.) – do not attempt to ice your cake unless you know that you are brilliant at it!

9 white columns to support the cakes

CAKE

1.5kg/3.3lb/10 cups of raisins

1kg/2.2lb/7 cups of dried currants

500g/17oz/3 cups of dried pineapple, chopped

600g/1lb 5oz/7cups of glacé cherries, halved

500g/17oz/3 cups of dried figs, chopped

400g/14oz/4½ cups of candied citrus peel, chopped

250g/8½oz/1¾ cups of stoned (pitted) dates, chopped

600g/1lb 5oz/4½ cups of rice flour

600g/1lb 5oz/4½ cups of millet flour

1 teaspoon of salt

2 tablespoons of mixed spice (pie spice)

1 tablespoon of grated nutmeg

2 tablespoons of ground allspice

1 tablespoon of ground cinnamon

1.1kg/2lb 6oz/4¾ cups of very soft, (DF) sunflower margarine and extra for greasing paper

1.2kg/2lb 10oz/6 cups of brown sugar

20 large free-range eggs

24 tablespoons of brandy

255g/9oz/2 cups of whole blanched almonds, roughly chopped

Grated rind of 2 oranges

CAKE COVERING

A normal sized jar of smooth apricot jam (jelly)

4 x 500g/17oz packets of ready-made to roll (GF) golden marzipan

Extra icing (confectioners') sugar for rolling

ICING

This is the icing recipe that I used, but most traditional royal icing recipes will be gluten and dairy free so these could be used as an alternative if you prefer.

4 medium free-range egg whites

800g/1lb 12oz/5½ cups of (GF) white icing (confectioners') sugar, sifted

1 tablespoon of lemon juice

1 teaspoon of glycerine

FOR EACH BATCH OF ICING (You will need three batches for the whole cake and may need a fourth if you are doing ornate decoration)

Beat the egg whites until slightly frothy in a food processor. Add the icing (confectioners') sugar, lemon juice and glycerine and beat until smooth.
Transfer the icing to a bowl and keep covered until needed, but do use it as quickly as you can.

Preheat the oven to 150°C/300°F/Gas mark 2

First make the cakes. Pour just enough boiling water over all the fruit in 2 huge bowls. Leave until the fruit becomes tepid. Drain and set the bowls of fruit to one side.
Meanwhile, grease and line the three cake tins with a double layer of baking parchment (wax paper) and then grease the paper for extra protection.
Sift the flours with the salt, mixed spice (pie spice), nutmeg, allspice and cinnamon into another huge bowl.
In another enormous bowl, bucket or jam (jelly) pan, cream together the margarine and sugar until soft and light.
Add 4 eggs at a time to this margarine mixture until you have added all the eggs. Now, gently mix in the flour and spices. Finally, add the brandy, dried fruits, nuts and grated orange.
Spoon this batter into the prepared cake tins and smooth over the tops, hollowing the centres slightly to prevent the cake rising and splitting in the centre.

Wrap double layers of foil around the outside of each cake tin and loosely cover the top of the cakes with foil. This will help to prevent the sides and top of the cake from burning while the centre of the cake is still undercooked.

Now begin baking (allow up to 6 hours baking time if you are planning to go out for the evening, that way none of the cakes will be hurried and undercooked).
Bake the largest cake for at least 4 hours or until an inserted skewer comes out clean from the centre of the cake (this could be as much as 5 hours if your oven is not as hot as mine is!). The second size cake should take about 3 hours, and the smallest cake should take about 1 1/2 hours (test both with a skewer as before – test them all in several places for reliability).

Leave the cakes to cool in their tins for 24 hours, then remove the cakes from the tins and peel off the baking parchment (wax paper). Wrap the cakes in foil and store in airtight containers for at least 2 weeks, but preferably for 2 months, before the wedding. Choose a cool place to let the cakes develop and mature nicely.

A week before the wedding, unwrap the cakes and place them in the centre of their corresponding sized silver boards. Make sure they are in the centre as you won't be able to move them later!

Cover the cakes in jam (jelly). Gently heat the apricot jam (jelly) in a bowl in the microwave and then brush the jam (jelly) all over the top and sides of the cakes. This seals the cakes and holds down the marzipan.

Now marzipan the cakes. (I used 2 blocks of marzipan to cover the large cake, 1 1/4 blocks for the middle size cake and 3/4 of a block for the smallest cake. The marzipan was not too thick but was not so thin that you could see the dark fruit underneath).

Sprinkle a work surface with icing (confectioners') sugar and roll out each block of marzipan with a rolling pin. When it is the correct thickness, use the rolling pin to lift the marzipan over the whole cake (the marzipan will stick to the jam (jelly) immediately so make sure you aim accurately).

If you can not cover the cake with one piece of marzipan, roll out smaller pieces to fill in any part of the cake that is not covered. You can mould it gently with your fingers so that it all blends in together and looks nice and smooth. It is most important to cover the cake completely so that the fruit will remain moist.

Trim off any excess marzipan and press closely to the cake. Trim again if necessary. Leave the cake for 24 hours to dry out in a cool place.

Repeat this with the remaining two cakes.

After 24 hours, when all three cakes will be ready, you can start icing the base cake first, or take the cakes to be iced and decorated.

Ice the cake. Make up the icing (1 batch at a time) and spread over each cake so that they are completely covered with icing and perfectly smooth and even all over.

Leave them to set hard before starting to decorate the cake. (Remember to wipe clean the silver boards before the icing sets).

When the icing is completely hard and set, make up a final batch of icing for the decoration and pipe your chosen design on to the cakes (you can add a little colour to the batch of icing you use for decorating the cake, if you wish, pale pink, pale blue or pale yellow can be used, but I kept mine all white).

Once all the icing has set, take the cake to the reception and assemble it. Put 1 column in the centre of the largest cake, and then 4 more columns, positioned to support the middle size cake on top of the base cake. Repeat with the remaining 4 columns to support the smallest cake on top of the middle cake.

Finally, decorate the cakes with flowers and ribbons. Don't forget the cake knife!

Easter Simnel Cake

This traditional Easter cake is not served at any other time of the year. I have never come across it anywhere other than England. Apparently, the 11 balls of marzipan signify the 11 Apostles of Jesus – Judas was not counted.

Serves 8–16

170g/6oz/³/₄ cup of (DF) margarine

170g/6oz/generous ³/₄ cup of caster (superfine) sugar

3 whole large free-range eggs and 1 egg white

115g/4oz/³/₄ cup of rice flour

115g/4oz/³/₄ cup of maize flour

Pinch of salt

1 heaped teaspoon of ground cinnamon

1 teaspoon of freshly grated nutmeg

100g/3¹/₂oz/¹/₂ cup of glacé cherries, cut into quarters

55g/2oz/¹/₃ cup of cut mixed peel, chopped

255g/9oz/1³/₄ cups of currants

100g/3¹/₂oz/³/₄ cups of sultanas (golden raisins)

Finely grated rind of 1 lemon

Lemon juice if necessary

500g/1lb 1oz of ready to roll (GF) marzipan

130g/4¹/₂oz of ready to roll (GF) marzipan, for the 11 decorative balls

Baking parchment (wax paper) and string

Grease an 18cm/7 inch, round cake tin and line with baking parchment (wax paper)

Ribbon to decorate the cake

Preheat the oven to 150°C/300°F/Gas mark 2

Beat the margarine and sugar in a food processor until fluffy. Transfer the mixture to a large bowl. In another bowl, lightly whisk the whole eggs, then gradually beat them into the creamed ingredients.

Sift the flours, salt and spices over the surface and fold into the mixture using a metal spoon. Add all the fruit and the lemon rind, folding together to give a smooth dropping consistency. If the mixture is too firm, add a little more lemon juice.

Divide the 500g/1lb 1oz marzipan in half. Lightly dust a surface with the icing (confectioners') sugar and roll out one half to a 16cm/6¹/₂ inch circle.

Spoon half the cake mixture into the prepared tin. Place the round of marzipan on top and cover with the remaining cake mixture. Press down gently with the back of a spoon to level the surface. Tie a double thickness of baking parchment (wax paper) round the outside of the tin. Bake in the oven for about 2¹/₂ hours. When it is cooked the cake should be a rich brown colour and firm to the touch. Cool in the tin for about 1 hour and then turn it out. Ease off the baking parchment (wax paper) and leave to cool completely on a wire rack.

Roll the remaining marzipan into a 16cm/6¹/₂ inch circle.

Lightly beat the egg white in a small bowl and brush a little of it over the top of the cake. Place the circle of marzipan on top of the cake and crimp the edges with your fingertips.

Use the 125g/4¹/₂oz of marzipan make eleven small balls. Use the palm of your clean hands to make the balls smooth and even.

Fix the eleven balls around the top edge of the cake with a little more of the beaten egg white.

Brush the marzipan with the remaining egg white and place under a hot grill for 1–2 minutes until the paste is well browned.

Tie a ribbon around the cake and store in an airtight container for up to a week.

Rosewater Angel Cake with Berries

Banana and Coffee Roulade

Marbled Peach Cheesecake

Chocolate and Pistachio Bavarois with Orange Sherry Sauce

Chocolate Shortbread Fingers and Valentine Hearts

Chocolate Marshmallow Crispies and Children's Cup Cakes

Marsala and Pecan Cake

Chocolate Dipped Strawberries

Children's Cup Cakes

Baking with the help of children in the kitchen is always fun and very messy – this is no exception!

Makes 12

130g/4½oz/½ cup plus 1 tablespoon of (DF) margarine, softened

130g/4½oz/½ cup plus 1 tablespoon of caster (superfine) sugar

2 large free-range eggs

125g/4½oz/generous ¾ cup of (WF) The Stamp Collection flour

1 teaspoon of Madagascan vanilla extract

2 heaped teaspoons of (GF) baking powder

A choice of food colourings, according to your taste

Icing (confectioners') sugar, sifted (about 200g/7oz/1⅓ cups in total)

12 glacé cherries or angelica slices or silver balls (check they are all suitable)

Line a 12, non-stick, bun-tray with paper cases

Preheat the oven to 200°C/400°F/Gas mark 6

Beat the margarine and the sugar together until light and fluffy in the food processor. Transfer the mixture to a bowl and fold in the eggs and flour half at a time. Gently fold in the vanilla and baking powder.

Divide the mixture between the paper cases and cook for 12–15 minutes, or until golden brown. Cool the cup cakes on a wire rack.

Now make the icing. You can make several different coloured icings by mixing a few drops of pink, yellow or green food colouring to suit your decoration. For example, pink icing with the cherries and yellow icing with angelica or green icing with silver balls.

Stir the icing (confectioners') sugar with the chosen colour and a little water in a small bowl until the icing is thick and smooth. Do not make it runny or the icing will drip off the cakes.

Spread the icing on each cake and decorate. Leave the icing to set before devouring the cakes. Store any that are left in an airtight container.

Dark Ginger Cake

I love really sticky gingerbread, so this is perfect. It is very useful for picnics or packed lunches as it does not crumble and has no icing or filling which can attach itself to anybody or anything.

Serves 8

140g/5oz/½ cup plus 2 tablespoons of (DF) margarine

140g/5oz/¾ cup of dark Mauritian sugar

2 large free-range eggs

115g/4oz/¾ cup of rice flour

115g/4oz/¾ cup of potato flour

285g/10oz/¾ cup of black treacle (molasses)

100g/3½oz/⅔ cup of plump sultanas (golden raisins)

2 heaped teaspoons of ground ginger

100g/3½oz/½ cup of chopped stem ginger

1 tablespoon of ginger wine

1 teaspoon of bicarbonate of soda (baking soda)

A greased square 23cm/9 inch cake tin, lined with baking parchment (wax paper)

Preheat the oven to 170°C/325°F/Gas mark 3

In a food processor, beat the margarine and sugar together until pale and creamy. Transfer to a large bowl, beat in the eggs and then add the flours, black treacle (molasses), sultanas (golden raisins), ground ginger and chopped ginger. Add the wine and bicarbonate of soda (baking soda) and mix thoroughly.

Put the mixture into the prepared tin and bake for about 1 hour. Reduce the heat to 150°C/300°F/Gas mark 2, cover the gingerbread with greased baking parchment (wax paper) and bake for another 45 minutes.

Leave the cake in the tin for 20 minutes and then turn out, upside down on to a wire rack to cool. When the cake is cold, peel off the baking parchment (wax paper), wrap the gingerbread in foil and store in an airtight container for up to a week.

Apple Cake

In England all sorts of irresistible apples are grown and we should all make more use of the wide choice available. Sadly most ancient varieties have been lost but some survive which date back to Anglo-Saxon times and retain their original 14th-century names.

Serves 8

130g/4½oz/generous ¾ cup of rice flour

130g/4½oz/generous ¾ cup of millet flour

A pinch of salt

2 teaspoons of (GF) baking powder

55g/2oz/⅔ cup of ground almonds

100g/3½oz/½ cup of caster (superfine) sugar (plus 1 tablespoon extra)

200g/7oz/1 cup less 2 tablespoons of (DF) margarine

455g/1lb/4 cups dessert apples, peeled and cored, half roughly chopped for inside the cake and half sliced for the top of the cake

2 large free-range eggs, beaten

2 tablespoons of cider or apple juice

40g/1½oz/3 tablespoons of brown sugar

1 teaspoon of ground cinnamon

55g/2oz/½ cup of slivered (flaked) almonds

Oil and line a deep 23cm/9-inch square cake tin

Baking parchment (wax paper)

Preheat the oven to 180°C/350°F/Gas mark 4

First, sift the flours, the salt and baking powder into a large bowl and stir in the ground almonds and caster (superfine) sugar. Add 170g/6oz/¾ cup of the margarine and rub in with your fingertips until the mixture resembles breadcrumbs.

Stir in the roughly chopped apples and beaten eggs. Add the cider and then spoon the mixture into the tin.

Neatly arrange all the sliced apples on top and sprinkle with 1 tablespoon of caster (superfine) sugar.

Bake for 45 minutes, or until the cake is just firm and the apples well browned. If the apples start to burn, cover the cake loosely with foil until the cake is just cooked through.

Meanwhile, heat the rest of the margarine, the brown sugar and the cinnamon together in a pan until it dissolves. Stir in the slivered (flaked) almonds.

Take the cake out of the oven and spread with the almond mixture. Return it to the oven to bake for a further 10 minutes, or until an inserted skewer comes out clean.

Leave the cake in the tin for 30 minutes, then turn out on to a serving plate and remove all the baking parchment (wax paper). Serve the cake cold.

Honey and Rosewater Roll

This is also delicious filled with (DF) vanilla ice-cream and crushed raspberries or strawberries and served immediately with a soft fruit purée.

Serves 10

ROLL

4 large free-range eggs, separated

115g/4oz/generous ¾ cup of icing (confectioners')
   sugar and extra for sprinkling

1 tablespoon of rosewater

55g/2oz/scant ½ cup of rice flour

55g/2oz/scant ⅓ cup of potato flour

1 teaspoon of (GF) baking powder

FILLING

3 tablespoons of scented runny honey

1 teaspoon of rosewater

100g/3½oz/7 tablespoons of (DF) margarine

100g/3½oz/¾ cup of icing (confectioners') sugar,
   sifted

Raspberry jam (jelly)

A clean tea towel

33cm/13 inch x 23cm/9 inch non-stick Swiss roll/
   roulade tin, completely lined with one piece of
   baking parchment (wax paper)

Preheat the oven to 190°C/375°F/Gas mark 5

First make the roll. In a large bowl, beat the egg whites with an electric whisk until they form soft peaks. Gradually sift and fold in half the icing (confectioners') sugar until the mixture stands in firm peaks.

In another bowl, beat the egg yolks and the remaining icing (confectioners') sugar until very thick. Stir in the rosewater. Gently fold in the flours and baking powder.

Lightly fold in the egg whites using a metal spoon, a third at a time, until all the egg whites are used up.

Lightly spread the mixture into the prepared tin and bake for 12 minutes until firm and springy when touched.

Sift and sprinkle the extra icing (confectioners') sugar on to a clean tea towel. Turn the cake on to the tea towel and carefully pull off the baking parchment (wax paper).

Cut any crisp edges off the cake, then roll up the cake in the tea towel and leave until it is cold.

Now make the filling. Beat the honey, rosewater, margarine and icing (confectioners') sugar together until smooth and spreadable (I usually use the food processor).

Carefully unroll the cake and spread it with as much or as little of the jam (jelly) as you like.

Lightly spread the filling over the raspberry jam (jelly) and roll up the cake.

Transfer the Swiss roll to a serving plate and dust it with extra sifted icing (confectioners') sugar.

Earl Grey Tea Loaf

This is a delightfully old-fashioned fruit loaf and as it improves with a few days in the cake tin, it is ideal for busy weekend entertaining or picnics.

Serves 8

140g/5oz/¹/₂ cup plus 2 tablespoons of (DF) margarine

170g/6oz/generous ³/₄ cup of caster (superfine) sugar

240ml/8fl oz/1 cup of strong Earl Grey tea

255g/9oz/1¹/₂ cups of dried mixed fruit, glacé pineapple, cherries, sultanas (golden raisins) or raisins

100g/3¹/₂oz/²/₃ cup of rice flour

100g/3¹/₂oz/²/₃ cup of potato flour

2 teaspoons of (GF) baking powder

Finely grated zest and juice of 1 lemon

1 large free-range egg, beaten

70g/2¹/₂oz/²/₃ cup of coarsely chopped walnuts

A little demerara sugar for sprinkling

Grease and line the base of a 25cm/10 inch × 10cm/ 4 inch loaf tin

Preheat the oven to 180°C/350°F/Gas mark 4

Put the margarine, sugar, tea and fruit in a saucepan, bring slowly to the boil and simmer for 5 minutes, stirring occasionally. Remove the saucepan from the heat and, when the mixture is cool, sift the flours and baking powder into the fruit mixture and mix it all together. Fold in the lemon zest and juice, the beaten egg and walnuts.

Pour the mixture into the prepared tin, sprinkle with the demarara sugar and bake for about 1–1¹/₂ hours, until well risen and firm in the centre. Leave the loaf in the tin to cool, then turn on to a wire rack to cool.

Store in an airtight container until needed. Serve the loaf sliced.

Fruit Cake

This recipe makes two fruit cakes so that one can be frozen for another time. If you are entertaining lots of people then you can make this as one large fruitcake, which will take an extra hour to cook.

Serves 10 (2 cakes), or 20 (1 large cake)

1kg/2.2lb/7 cups of mixed dried fruit such as sultanas (golden raisins), currants, mixed peel, glacé cherries and pineapple

100ml/3½ fl oz/⅓ cup of Amaretto di Saronno liqueur

300ml/10fl oz/1¼ cups of orange juice

100ml/3½ fl oz/½ cup of coconut cream

Grated zest of 1 orange

6 large free-range eggs, separated

225g/8oz/1 generous cup of dark brown soft sugar

140g/5oz/⅔ cup of unsweetened canned chestnut purée

225g/8oz/1 cup of (DF) margarine, softened

115g/4oz/1⅓ cups of ground almonds

115g/4oz/¾ cup of rice flour

70g/2½oz/½ cup of whole blanched almonds to decorate (or more for a more luxurious look)

2 x 20cm/8-inch square non-stick cake tins at least 9cm/3½ inch deep, lined with baking parchment (wax paper)

Kitchen foil

Preheat the oven to 170°C/325°F/Gas mark 3

If you have time, it is a great idea to macerate the fruit 24 hours in advance. To do this, put all the dried fruit, Amaretto, orange juice and coconut cream together in a very large bowl with the grated orange. Mix well to blend the liquids and coat the fruit. Cover the bowl and keep in a cool place until needed.

To make the cake, put the egg yolks, soft brown sugar, chestnut purée and margarine in the food processor and blend until fluffy. Transfer to a very large bowl. Sift the ground almonds and the rice flour into the mixture and fold in. Stir in the prepared dried fruit and all the liquid.

Whisk the egg whites in a bowl until they are stiff and then fold them into the fruit mixture.

Divide the mixture between the 2 tins and decorate with the whole almonds.

Bake in the oven for 2½ hours or until the cakes are firm and cooked all the way through. You will probably need to cover the cakes with foil half way through the cooking so that the cakes do not burn. If the sides seem to be getting too dark then wrap foil around the tins as well and cook for a little longer to make sure the centre is cooked through.

Leave the cakes to cool in the tins and then turn them out and remove all the paper.

Serve the cake when it is cold and store it in an airtight container until needed.

Macadamia Nut Pound Cake

Make this cake the day before you need it so that the flavours have time to develop.

Serves 8

70g/2¹/₂oz/¹/₂ cup of macadamia nuts

Extra rice flour

70g/2¹/₂oz/¹/₂ cup of polenta (maize)

130g/4¹/₂oz/generous ³/₄ cup of rice flour

1 heaped teaspoon of GF baking powder

¹/₂ teaspoon of bicarbonate of soda (baking soda)

A pinch of salt

140g/5oz/1 cup of icing (confectioners') sugar

130g/4¹/₂oz/¹/₂ cup plus 1 tablespoon of DF margarine

2 large free-range eggs, beaten

100ml/3¹/₂ fl oz/¹/₃ cup of goat's or sheep's yogurt

3 tablespoons of maple syrup

Grease a 23cm/9 inch, round or square, deep-sided, loose-bottomed, non-stick, cake tin and line it with baking parchment (wax paper)

Preheat the oven to 190°C/375°F/Gas mark 5

Put the nuts on a non-stick baking sheet and cook them in the oven until golden. Roughly chop up the nuts and sprinkle with a little bit of extra rice flour.

Sift together the polenta (maize), flour, baking powder, bicarbonate of soda (baking soda) and salt into a large bowl.

Beat the icing (confectioners') sugar and margarine in a food processor until pale and fluffy. Add the eggs and half the flour mixture and mix briefly. Add the yogurt, maple syrup, nuts and the rest of the flour mixture and blend very briefly.

Spoon into the prepared cake tin and bake for 40 minutes, or until brown and firm to touch. An inserted skewer should come out clean when the cake is cooked.

Leave the cake to cool in the tin, then peel off the baking parchment (wax paper) and leave the cake to go cold on a wire rack.

Wrap the cake in clingfilm (plastic wrap) or keep it in an airtight container until needed.

Marsala and Pecan Cake

This is very much a grown-up cake, the sort you get at afternoon tea in a smart London hotel. However, if you are not a tea drinker then a double espresso and a slice of this cake is a real treat at any time of the day.

Serves 8–12

CAKE

4 large free-range eggs, separated and 1 extra egg
   white
140g/5oz/³/₄ cup of caster (superfine) sugar
200g/7oz/1³/₄ cups of pecan nuts
4 heaped tablespoons of 100% rye breadcrumbs
¹/₂ a heaped teaspoon of cream of tartar

MARSALA ICING

225g/8oz/1 cup of (DF) margarine, softened
255g/9oz/1³/₄ cups of icing (confectioners') sugar,
   sifted
75ml/2¹/₂ fl oz/¹/₄ cup of Marsala
Pecan halves to decorate
(GF) cocoa powder to dust

Grease and line with baking parchment (wax paper) a
   20 cm/8 inch non-stick, loose-bottomed, cake tin
   with deep sides

Preheat the oven to 180°C/350°F/Gas mark 4

Make the cake first. Beat the egg yolks and sugar together in the food processor until pale and fluffy. Add the nuts and process briefly, so that they are finely chopped. Add the breadcrumbs and mix together for a moment. Transfer the mixture into a large bowl.

In another bowl, beat the egg whites with the extra egg white and the cream of tartar until stiff. Fold 2 tablespoons of the egg whites into the pecan mixture and then gently fold in the rest. Spoon the mixture into the cake tin and bake for about 35 minutes, or until firm and brown and well risen.

Leave the cake to cool in the tin for 20 minutes, then turn it out and peel off the baking parchment (wax paper). Allow the cake cool on a wire rack.

Now make the icing. Beat the margarine and icing (confectioners') sugar until light and fluffy in the food processor, then carefully add a little Marsala at a time. Do not over beat or it will separate, also take care not to add too much Marsala as this will also make it separate.

Slice the cake in half horizontally and when it is cold, spread the sponge with about one third of the icing. Cover with the top of the cake and spread the rest of the icing all over the cake. Decorate the top of the cake with pecan halves and dust with sifted cocoa powder.

Store in an airtight container in the refrigerator until needed.

Coconut and Lime Cake

This light summery cake tastes fresh and zingy, just what I love on a hot summer's day with a glass of iced tea and lemon.

Serves 8–10

CAKE
170g/6oz/³/₄ cup of (DF) margarine, softened

170g/6oz/generous ³/₄ cup of caster (superfine) sugar

Grated zest of 2 limes and their juice

4 large free-range eggs, separated

100g/3¹/₂oz/²/₃ cup of rice flour, sifted

100g/3¹/₂oz/²/₃ cup of millet flour, sifted

Pinch of salt

1 heaped teaspoon of (GF) baking powder

55g/2oz/²/₃ cup of desiccated (shredded) coconut

240g/8fl oz/1 cup of goat's or sheep's natural yogurt

¹/₂ teaspoon of cream of tartar

ICING
3 ripe passion fruit, halved and flesh scooped into a bowl

Juice of ¹/₂ a lime

170g/6oz/1¹/₄ cups of sifted icing (confectioners') sugar or more if the mixture is too runny

Grease and line with baking parchment (wax paper) a 23cm/9 inch, non-stick, deep-sided, loose-bottomed cake tin

Preheat the oven to 180°C/350°F/Gas mark 4

Make the cake first. Beat the margarine and sugar in a food processor, then beat in the lime zest and egg yolks. Transfer the mixture to a bowl and fold in the flours with the salt, baking powder and coconut. Fold in the lime juice and yogurt. Whisk the cream of tartar with the egg whites until stiff in another bowl.

Fold the egg whites into the cake mixture and spoon into the prepared cake tin.

Bake in the oven for about 45 minutes, or until golden brown, firm and springy to touch.

Cool the cake in the tin for 10 minutes, then turn out and peel off the baking parchment (wax paper). Leave the cake to cool on a wire rack.

Meanwhile, make the icing. Mix the passion fruit pulp with the lime juice and beat in the icing (confectioners') sugar using a wooden spoon. Add more icing (confectioners') sugar if the icing is too runny (this will depend on the size of passion fruit and lime you are using and how ripe and juicy they are).

Place the cake on a serving plate and spread the icing over the top of the cake. Leave to set in a cool place.

Keep the cake in an airtight container in the refrigerator until needed.

Rhubarb and Orange Cake

It had never occurred to me to use rhubarb in a cake so I was astonished when I saw a recipe for one. Cinnamon, rhubarb and nuts are remarkably good together and it is an excellent way of using up leftover rhubarb.

Serves 8–12

CAKE

255g/9oz/1 ¾ cups of washed, trimmed and dried
    rhubarb, cut into 4cm/1 ½inch lengths
200g/7oz/1 cup of caster (superfine) sugar
Finely grated zest and the juice of 1 orange
140g/5oz/½ cup plus 2 tablespoons of (DF)
    margarine, softened
2 large free-range eggs
85g/3oz/9 tablespoons of rice flour
1 teaspoon of (GF) baking powder
100g/3½oz/1 cup of desiccated (shredded) coconut

1 teaspoon of ground cinnamon

TOPPING

30g/1oz/2 tablespoons of (DF) margarine
30g/1oz/2 tablespoons of caster (superfine) sugar
85g/3oz/¾ cup of slivered (flaked) almonds
1 teaspoon of ground cinnamon

Grease and line with baking parchment (wax paper)
a 20cm/8 inch, deep-sided, loose-bottomed, non-stick
cake tin

Preheat the oven to 180°C/350°F/Gas mark 4

Put the rhubarb into a bowl with 55g/2oz/¼ cup of the sugar, the orange zest and juice. Mix well and then cook in the microwave for about 4 minutes, or until the rhubarb is just cooked and all the juices have seeped out.

Drain the rhubarb in a sieve and keep the juice for something else as it is too good to waste!

In another bowl, beat the margarine and the remaining sugar together until light and fluffy. Stir in the eggs, flour, baking powder, coconut and cinnamon as lightly and quickly as possible.

Mix the rhubarb into the cake mixture and transfer to the prepared tin. Bake in the oven for about 40 minutes until well browned and fairly firm.

Meanwhile, melt all the topping ingredients together in a saucepan and stir over very low heat, until the nuts are evenly coated.

Take the cake out of the oven and spread the nut mixture over the top of the cake.

Return the cake to the oven and bake for another 20 minutes. The cake should now be firm and springy to touch.

Leave the cake to cool in the tin for about 1 hour and then turn it on to a wire rack and remove the baking parchment (wax paper).

Serve in thick chunks and store any leftovers wrapped in clingfilm (plastic wrap) in an airtight container.

Walnut and Chocolate Cake

This is hugely indulgent and wicked! A double bonus of chocolate in the cake and in the icing as well. This is particularly suitable for chocolate indulgence at Easter.

Serves 8

CAKE
140g/5oz/¹/₂ cup plus 2 tablespoons (DF) margarine, softened
140g/5oz/³/₄ cup of caster (superfine) sugar
2 large free-range eggs, beaten
100g/3¹/₂oz/²/₃ cup of rice flour, sifted
30g/1oz/¹/₃ cup of ground almonds
Pinch of salt
1 heaped teaspoon of (GF) baking powder
85g/3oz of (DF) dark chocolate, coarsely chopped or grated
115g/4oz/1¹/₃ cups of walnut halves, as fresh as possible, roughly chopped
1 tablespoon of strong black coffee

ICING
100g/3¹/₂oz of continental (DF) dark chocolate
30g/1oz/2 tablespoons of (DF) margarine
85g/3oz/1 cup of walnut halves, as fresh as possible

Grease and line with baking parchment (wax paper) an 20cm/8-inch square, loose-bottomed, deep-sided, non-stick cake tin

Preheat the oven to 180°C/350°F/Gas mark 4

Cream the margarine and sugar in a food processor until pale and fluffy. Gradually add the eggs, flour, almonds and salt, mixing only very briefly. Transfer the mixture to a large bowl and fold in the baking powder, chopped chocolate, chopped walnuts and coffee.

Spoon the mixture into the prepared tin and bake for 30 minutes, or until firm to the touch. Cool the cake for 15 minutes in the tin and then lift it out, remove the base with the baking parchment (wax paper) and place it topside up on to a wire rack until cold. Peel the baking parchment (wax paper) off the sides of the cake.

Melt the chocolate for the icing with the margarine in a small bowl in the microwave and stir it until it is smooth.

Spread the icing over the top of the cake and once it has set, arrange the whole walnut halves all over the cake.

Cut the cake into squares or bars and keep it in an airtight container until needed.

Chocolate Truffles

These truffles could not be easier to make and are such a treat for birthdays, Christmas and Easter. Serve them in little gold paper cases with coffee after dinner parties or just spoil yourself when you have a lust for chocolate!

Serves 10 (2 each)

255g/9oz/1½ cups of luxury dark (DF) chocolate
55g/2oz/¼ cup of (DF) margarine
75ml/2½ fl oz/¼ cup of soya cream
Brandy, Cognac or Cointreau (or 1 teaspoon of pure

Madagascan vanilla extract and 1 teaspoon of warm
water or black coffee, if no alcohol is desired)
(DF) Cocoa powder

Break the chocolate into a bowl, add the margarine and melt briefly in the microwave.
Stir in the cream and mix well together. Add the brandy or liqueur, or the vanilla and coffee mixture, and stir together until smooth.
Leave to cool and when the mixture is firm, mould teaspoons of the chocolate into balls in your hands. Roll the balls in cocoa powder and leave in the refrigerator to set.
(Alternatively, roll them in browned nuts and chill until needed).
Slip the truffles into little foil or paper cases and serve cool but not rock hard and cold.
You can arrange them in a pretty box, tied up with a ribbon to give as a gift – these truffles need to be kept chilled, so please ask the lucky recipient to keep them in the refrigerator until shortly before needed!

Fondant Cape Gooseberries

The sweet, fondant coating perfectly complements the small explosion of tart juices. You can dip the Cape gooseberries (physalis) in (DF) caramel or (DF) luxury chocolate.

Serves 10 (4 each)

40 ripe Cape gooseberries (physalis)

140g/5oz/1 cup of sifted icing (confectioners') sugar

1 tablespoon of orange liqueur

1 tablespoon of freshly squeezed orange juice

A few drops of food colouring, optional

1 large plate or tray with about 2 tablespoons of sifted icing (confectioners') sugar sprinkled over it

Hold the stalks of the Cape gooseberries (physalis) and gently open out the papery lanterns that conceal the berries. Fold the wings right back, giving them a little twist as you do so.

In a small bowl, beat the icing (confectioners') sugar with the liqueur and orange juice until smooth. Stir in a couple of drops of food colouring if desired, or divide the mixture in half and colour one half, leaving the other plain.

Holding the wings of the fruit carefully, dip the berries into the icing until evenly covered. Allow the excess to drip off before placing it on to the prepared plate or tray.

Keep in a cool place (not the refrigerator) and eat within 48 hours.

Chocolate-dipped Strawberries

The ultimate luxury must be the combination of fresh strawberries and bitter chocolate. A very sensual and easy pudding for St. Valentine's night, or an ideal treat for the calorie-conscious chocolate lover! For just two of you, halve the quantities in the recipe.

Serves 4 (5 each)

20 large ripe strawberries

140g/5oz/scant cup of luxury (DF) dark continental
   chocolate

A few drops of sunflower oil

A large plate sprinkled with sieved (DF) cocoa
   powder

Kitchen (paper) towels

Wash the strawberries and carefully dry them on kitchen (paper) towels.

Microwave the chocolate in a small bowl with a couple of drops of oil until just melted and then stir until smooth.

Dip the strawberries into the chocolate and let any excess chocolate drip off.

Place on the prepared plate and chill until needed.

Serve the strawberries on a glass or silver dish for special occasions and devour them within 48 hours.

Peppermint Creams

If you don't like chocolate but love peppermint these are perfect for you. They are so easy to prepare that children can make them as presents.

Makes lots!

455g/1lb/3 cups of icing (confectioners') sugar, sifted	1 large free-range egg white, lightly whisked
1 teaspoon of lemon juice	1 teaspoon of peppermint flavouring or oil
2 teaspoons of water	Green food colouring, optional

Mix the sugar with the lemon juice, water and enough egg white to make a pliable mixture. Divide the mixture in half and flavour one half with peppermint and a few drops of green food colouring and the other half with only the peppermint flavouring.

Knead on a clean surface, dusted with icing (confectioners') sugar, and then gently roll out each mixture separately into a long sausage.

Slice the dough into neat little rounds or form into balls and flatten slightly with the back of a fork.

Leave the peppermint creams somewhere safe and cool for 24 hours until thoroughly dry. You can pack them into little paper cases and put them into a pretty box or keep the peppermint creams in an air-tight container until needed.

Walnut and Pecan Creams

Another easy, though slightly more sophisticated recipe which children can make and give as presents.

Makes lots!

455g/1lb/3 cups of icing (confectioners') sugar, sifted

1 teaspoon of lemon juice

1 large free-range egg white, lightly whisked

1 dessertspoon of coffee essence

1 teaspoon of water

At least 12 whole walnut halves

At least 12 whole pecan halves

100g/3½oz/½ cup dark (DF) luxury continental chocolate, optional

Mix the icing (confectioners') sugar, lemon juice and egg white in a bowl until pliable. Add the coffee essence and water. Knead on a clean surface dusted with icing (confectioners') sugar. Shape the mixture into balls about 2.5cm/1 inch in diameter, press half a walnut into half of the coffee balls and press the pecans into the remaining coffee balls (this should flatten the balls slightly).

For chocolate-drizzled creams, melt the chocolate in a small bowl in the microwave, stir until smooth and drizzle over the nuts on each sweet.

Put the walnut and pecan creams into little paper cases and leave them for 24 hours to set and dry. Transfer to a pretty box or keep them in an airtight container until needed.

My List of Ingredients

Lately, the biggest modern blight that disrupts social occasions is the ever-increasing list of foods to be avoided by children and adults of all ages. My recipes feature many familiar ingredients, but also staple foods such as soya products that you might normally hesitate to buy. The advantage of this little list is that you will be able to whip up some little concoction at a moment's notice. Respond to your culinary impulses and create something delicious and comforting.

Good quality sunflower and corn oil

Unsweetened apple juice

Ground almonds and other nuts

Cold pressed organic honey, treacle and Golden syrup (corn syrup)

High quality sugar free fruit jams (jelly)

Pure Madagascan vanilla extract

Dairy free luxury dark chocolate

100% pure dairy free cocoa powder

Soya milk, yogurt and cream

Dairy free sunflower and soya margarine

Frozen (DF) ice-cream dessert in different flavours

(Swedish Glace or Toffuti are excellent)

Amaretto di Saronno Liqueur, White Rum and Cointreau

Instant polenta (maize) and maize flour

Oats, buckwheat flour and rice flour

Gluten free cornflour (cornstarch), potato flour, millet flakes and flour

Gluten free baking powder and baking soda

Gluten free cream of tartar

Pudding rice and ground rice

Large free-range eggs

Unrefined brown Mauritian sugar and caster (superfine) sugar

Icing (confectioners') sugar

All sorts of mixed dried fruits

Ground mixed spice (pie spice), ginger and cinnamon

Coconut cream and milk

Frozen mixed berries

Jars of sweetened (with honey) apple purée

Sachets of powdered gelatine or vegetarian equivalent

Stem ginger in syrup

Gluten free ready made to roll marzipan

100% pure maple syrup

Please check your mixed spice (pie spice) is gluten free; if in doubt make up
    your own jar with single spices, seal and store.

Some Useful Addresses

United Kingdom

Institute for Optimum Nutrition
Blades Court
Deodar Road
London SW15 2NU
Telephone 0181 877 9993

Action Against Allergy
24–26 High Street
Hampton Hill
Middlesex TW1 1PD
Telephone 0181 892 2711

Coeliac Society
P O Box 220
High Wycombe
Buckinghamshire HP11 2HY
Telephone 01494437278

National Eczema Society
163 Evershalt Street
London NW1 1BU
Telephone 0171 388 4097

Myalgic Encephalomyelitis (ME) Society
PO Box 87
Stanford-le-Hope
Essex SS17 8EX
Telephone 01375 642466

United States of America

Allergy Resources Inc.
PO Box 888
Palmer Lake
CO 80133
Telephone 800 873 3529

British Heart Foundation
14 Fitzhardinge Street
London W1H 4DH
Telephone 0171 935 0185

IBS Network
Centre for Human Nutrition
Northern General Hospital
Sheffield S5 7AU
Telephone 01142611531

Nutrition Associates
Galtres House
Lysander Close
Clifton Moregate
York YO3 0XB
Telephone 01904 691591

Berrydales Publishers
Berrydale House
5 Lawn Road
London NW3 2XS
Telephone 0171 722 2866
(*The Inside Story* food & health magazine)

The Vegetarian Society
Parkdale
Dunham Road
Altrincham
Cheshire WA14 4QG
Telephone 01619 280793

American Allergy Association
PO Box 7273
Menlo Park
CA 94026
Telephone 415 322 1663

American Celiac Society
Dietary Support Coalition
Ms Annette Bentley
58 Musano Court
West Orange
NJ 07052

Asthma and Allergy Foundation of America
1717 Massachusetts Avenue
Suite 305
Washington DC 20036
Telephone 202 265 0265

Gluten Intolerance Group
PO Box 23053
Seattle
WA 98102
Telephone 206 854 9606

STOCKISTS

United Kingdom

The Fresh Food Company
326 Portobello Road
London W10 5RU
Telephone 0181 969 0351

Allergy Care
9 Coporation Street
Taunton
Somerset TA1 4AJ
Telephone 01823 325 023

D&D Chocolates
261 Forest Road
Loughborough
LE11 3HT
Telephone 01509 216 400

Farm-a-round Ltd
(Organic fruit and vegetables delivered to your door)
Forest House
4 Dartmouth Road
London SE23 3XU
Telephone 0181 291 4519

HR Higgins Ltd
(Decaffeinated teas and coffees)
79 Duke Street
London W1M 6AS
Telephone 0171 629 3913

Doves Farm Foods Ltd
(Wheat- and Gluten-free flours)
Salisbury Road
Hungerford
Berkshire RG17 0RF
Telephone 01488 684 880

USA Stockists

Arrowhead Mills Inc.
(Mail order suppliers of grains, flours, legumes, cereals and seeds.)
Box 2059
Hereford TX 79045
Telephone 800 749 0730
Fax 806 364 8242

Bob's Red Mill Natural Foods Inc.
(Mail order stockists of grains, flours, legumes, cereals and seeds.)
5209 SE International Way
Milwaukee
OR 97222
Telephone 503 654 3215
Fax 503 653 1339

Ener-g Foods Inc.
(Suppliers of food allergy products, many rice-based, including rice flours, rice pasta, egg substitute, almond milk mix as well as baked goods.)
PO Box 84487
Seattle
WA 98124-5787
Telephone 800 331 5222
Fax 206 764 3398

Gold Mine Natural Food Co.
(Stockist of rice, barley and other organic grains and seeds.)
3419 Hancock Street
San Diego

CA 92110-4307
Telephone 800 475 3663
Fax 619 296 9756

Jaffe Brothers Natural Foods
(Wholefood suppliers of nuts, nut butters, dried fruits and grains.)
PO Box 636
Valley Center
CA 92082 0636
Telephone 616 749 1133
Fax 619 749 1282

Mast Enterprises
265 North Fourth Street, #616
Coeur D'Alene
ID 83814
Telephone 208 772 8213

Mountain Ark Trader
(Suppliers of grains and 100% buckwheat noodles, Japanese-style silken tofu, soy milk and rice milk.)
PO Box 3170
Fayetteville
AR 72701
Telephone 800 647 8909
Fax 501 442 7191

Walnut Acres Organic Farms
Penns Creek
PA 17862
Telephone 800 433 3998
Fax 717 837 1146

Quick Reference Guide to Allergens

This quick reference guide will show you some of the ingredients that should be avoided by people suffering dairy, gluten or sugar intolerance

Dairy	Gluten	Sugar
Butter	Durum wheat (pasta)	Some sweeteners
Buttermilk	Barley	Honey
Cheese	Semolina	Fructose
Cream	Sausages	Sugar
Ghee	Malt	Maltose
Hydrolysed whey protein	Oats	Golden syrup (corn syrup)
Lactose	Wheat flour	Invert syrup
Margarine or shortening containing whey	Bran	Glucose (including glucose syrup)
Milk solids	Prepared stuffing	Molasses
Non-milk fat solids	Starch (including modified starch)	Maple syrup
Skimmed milk powder		Treacle
Whey	Rusk	Dextrose
Yogurt	Whisky	
	Beer	Corn syrup
		Malt syrup
	Mixed (pie) spice	Sucrose

As butter is tastier and may be healthier when heated than many margarines, I recommend using butter in place of margarine in the recipes if you can tolerate it.
However, do not try this unless you are sure you are able to tolerate butter.

Some brands of mixed (pie) spice containing gluten. If in doubt, you can make up our own jar with single, unadultered spices, seal and store.

Index of Recipes

Index

Antoinette Savill

THE SENSITIVE GOURMET
Cooking Without Wheat, Gluten or Dairy

A lavish hardback cookery book for the thousands of people suffering from sensitivity to wheat, dairy products and gluten (the elastic substance in wheat, oats and barley). Those with food allergies, ME, coeliac disease, asthma, eczema and dermatitis will find it invaluable.

This book is designed to bring back a pure enjoyment of food and the recipes are smart, modern, international and anything but depriving. From pear tatin to Thai soup with mussels, ginger and lemongrass, Antoinette Savill's cunning with such alternative ingredients as tofu, coconut milk and rice flour is second to none. Also includes menus for special occasions, from a Christmas feast to summer barbecues.

Thorsons

Directions for life